In theory, democratic government rests on the idea of popular sovereignty. Writing in 1798, James Madison envisioned an informed electorate actively participating in public policy debates. In practice, of course, democratic government doesn't often work that way. "The notion that the public really controls the government," writes columnist Anthony Lewis, "has always had elements of myth in it."

The recent presidential election campaign was widely regarded as an unsatisfying process, which often veered away from the matter of how the country should be governed toward highly personal questions about who would govern it. Some pressing national issues were barely addressed. Finding the whole process boring and irrelevant, many people have simply dropped out of electoral politics.

This sense of alienation from the electoral process is a symptom of deeper dissatisfactions with the democratic process, which have as much to do with our role as citizens as they do with how campaigns are run, or the actions of elected officials. It is not enough for us to sit in front of our televisions, watching political campaigns and listening to elected officials. Democracy is not, after all, a spectator sport.

As James Madison reminded his readers, a working democracy assumes that citizens are *active* participants. But participants in what, exactly? For the majority of us who do not hold public office, it is not clear how we can participate in public life, other than casting a vote and paying taxes. In many communities, no forums are held at which people discuss public issues.

The purpose of the National Issues Forums (NIF) — locally initiated Forums and study circles which bring citizens together in communities across the nation for nonpartisan discussion about public issues — is to provide a place for the practice of citizenship. In several respects, the NIF is intended to restore what's missing from the democratic process.

Since the word "citizen" is often used rhetorically, it may seem odd to think of the citizen's role as one that requires specific skills that have to be cultivated, like other skills. Yet the premise of the NIF is that the skills of public discourse — listening as well as talking about common problems and comparing different views of the public interest — are as important today as they were in the eighteenth century, when town meetings were a vital public institution.

Each year, convenors of NIF choose three issues for discussion. Since good talk requires a common framework and a certain familiarity with the issue, a book like this one is prepared for each topic. A distinctive feature of these books is that they present several choices. Citizens need to put themselves in the position of elected officials by considering various courses of action, and learning about their costs and consequences. An important aspect of what we refer to as "choicework" is to examine how our values as individuals and community members apply to a particular issue.

After the community Forums and study groups meet, the NIF convenes a series of meetings with national leaders to convey the outcome of these discussions. So that we can convey your thoughts and feelings about this issue, two ballots are included at the end of this book. Before you begin reading these materials and then after you've read them and taken part in Forums, I urge you to fill them out and mail them back to us.

This book, like the others in this series, is a guide to one of the nation's pressing issues and an invitation to engage in public discussion about it.

Keith Melville

Keith Melville, Editor-in-Chief

Editor-in-Chief: Keith Melville
Writer: Keith Melville
Research: Sophie Rosenfeld
Editor: Betty Frecker
Ballots: John Doble, Josh Klein, and
    Amy Richardson
Production Manager:
    George Cavanaugh
Production Director: Robert E. Daley

Designer: Sundberg, Morance &
    Associates Inc.
Circulation Coordinator:
    Victoria Simpson
Cover Illustration: Mirko Ilic
Word Processing: Valerie Braum
Formatting: Karen Bocko
Graphic Research: Sophie Rosenfeld

The books in this series are prepared by The Public Agenda Foundation — a nonprofit, nonpartisan organization devoted to research and education about public issues — and published jointly by the Kettering Foundation and the Kendall/Hunt Publishing Company. They are used by civic and educational organizations interested in addressing public issues.

In particular, they are used in local discussion groups that are part of a nationwide network, the National Issues Forums (NIF). The NIF consists of more than 1,300 civic and educational organizations — colleges and universities, libraries, service clubs, and membership groups. Although each community group is locally controlled, NIF is a collaborative effort. Each year, convenors choose three issues and use common materials — issue books such as this one, and parallel audio and videotape materials.

Groups interested in using the NIF materials and adapting its approach as part of their own program are invited to write or call for further information: National Issues Forums, 100 Commons Road, Dayton, Ohio 45459-2777. Phone 1-800-433-7834, in Ohio dial 1-800-433-4819.

The NIF issue books— both the standard edition and an abridged version at a lower reading level, as well as audiocassette and videocassette versions of the same material — can be ordered from Kendall/Hunt Publishing Company, 2460 Kerper Boulevard, Dubuque, Iowa 52004-0539. Phone 1-800-338-5578. The following titles are available:

The Day Care Dilemma: Who Should Be Responsible for the Children?
The Drug Crisis: Public Strategies for Breaking the Habit
The Environment at Risk: Responding to Growing Dangers
Health Care for the Elderly: Moral Dilemmas, Mortal Choices
Coping with AIDS: The Public Response to the Epidemic
The Public Debt: Breaking the Habit of Deficit Spending
The Superpowers: Nuclear Weapons and National Security
The Trade Gap: Regaining the Competitive Edge
Freedom of Speech: Where to Draw the Line
Crime: What We Fear, What Can Be Done
Immigration: What We Promised, Where to Draw the Line
The Farm Crisis: Who's in Trouble, How to Respond

ISBN 0-8403-5270-0

THE DRUG CRISIS: PUBLIC STRATEGIES FOR BREAKING THE HABIT

PREPARED BY THE PUBLIC AGENDA FOUNDATION

CONTENTS

THE GREAT DRUG DEBATE

"Lawmakers and the American public agree that the drug problem is getting worse and that anti-drug efforts are largely ineffective. What is likely to prove successful in stopping drugs?"

In mid-October 1988, in the final hours of the 100th Congress, members of the House and Senate prepared to return to their districts for election-year campaigning. But one last piece of legislative business kept them in the capital: reform of the nation's drug laws.

House and Senate leaders struggled to reach a compromise on a final version of drug legislation that had been in the works for months. In the midst of a presidential election campaign, members of Congress felt obliged to respond to public demands for action on the drug crisis. "Congress is afraid *not* to act on drugs," said Senator Arlen Specter. "It is not a matter of leadership. We are being pushed into it by an irate public."

Anti-drug measures are an election-year staple in Washington. In 1982, President Reagan announced a major new campaign against illicit drugs. Congress followed suit in 1984 and 1986 with additional anti-drug measures. As a result of those initiatives, federal expenditures on drug enforcement tripled between 1981 and 1987, rising from less than $1 billion to about $3 billion. Government expenditures on all aspects of drug enforcement in the United States — from the eradication of drugs in foreign countries to the prosecution and imprisonment of sellers and users in the United States — came to at least $10 billion in 1987.

However, despite that commitment to contain the spread of illicit drugs, and despite the arrests of some 800,000 Americans per year on drug-law violations there is little reason for optimism. As members of Congress considered comprehensive new measures in 1988, they didn't have to look far for disappointing news about the war on drugs.

Police in the District of Columbia have engaged for several years in one of the most aggressive anti-drug programs in the country. As a result of a widely publicized effort called Operation Clean Sweep, Washington has the highest rate of drug-related arrests of any major city in the United States. Still, the District's drug problem is getting worse. The city's residents are so concerned about the problem that local officials are constantly confronted by residents who demand additional anti-drug efforts. Throughout the country, public officials have been getting the same message.

EVERYONE'S PROBLEM

This new sense of urgency about the drug problem is fueled by media accounts about international drug thugs and street wars among drug dealers. On the international front, the media have featured stories about drug trafficking by Panama's military leader, General Manuel Antonio Noriega, and underworld mobs in South American nations such as Colombia, where drug kingpins appear to have subverted the political leadership of an entire nation.

Closer to home, newspapers in most American cities have devoted front-page coverage to drug-related crimes and violence. In the early 1980s, so-called "cocaine cowboys" made news when they terrorized Miami and other regions of south Florida. Now similar drug-related activity is common in many cities, such as Washington, D.C., where the local drug market is controlled by Jamaican gangs known as "posses." In New York City, law enforcement officials estimate that more than 4 out of 5 men arrested for criminal activity test positive for drugs, and roughly 40 percent of all homicides are linked to disputes or robberies involving drugs. In Los Angeles, escalating gang violence is blamed on turf battles between rival drug rings.

Meanwhile, quick profits from drug sales are corrupting the criminal justice system — including agents of the FBI and the Customs Service, as well as rural sheriffs who are charged with accepting bribes and dealing drugs themselves. State and federal courts have dealt with more than 100 cases in each of the past few years in which law enforcement officials are charged with drug corruption. In Miami, where the drug problem is particularly severe, several dozen members of the police department have come under investigation for drug trafficking.

Although the drug problem is most evident in inner-city neighborhoods, both drug use and drug-related crime are readily apparent in many communities. Today, drug use is a problem not only in the South Bronx and in Beverly Hills but in Middle America, too. In neighborhoods where drug use itself is uncommon, drug-related crime such as the theft of car radios by users who resort to such measures to support their habits is increasingly frequent. A national poll conducted by the *Washington Post* in March 1988 found that about half of all Americans said they had a relative or close friend who has a problem with illicit drugs.

As illicit drugs become more common throughout the country, the effects of drug use are readily apparent. According to White House drug adviser Donald Ian Macdonald, one in five American workers uses illegal drugs, which leads to absenteeism, higher accident rates, and a loss of productivity.

JIM MORIN, *THE MIAMI HERALD*

23 MILLION AMERICANS

Use of illicit drugs is a serious and pervasive problem. An estimated 20 million Americans use marijuana at least once a month. Four to eight million people are cocaine users. Half a million people are heroin addicts. In all, some 23 million Americans regularly buy and use illicit drugs.

It is not just the volume of the drug trade that is worrisome. Because the price of some of the most commonly used drugs has dropped, more people can afford to use them. Consequently, cocaine, which gained a certain prominence as the preferred drug of the rich and famous, can now be bought by people of modest means. In some cities, junior high school students pool their allowances to form "$12.50 clubs" to make small scores of cocaine.

Because the drugs sold today are particularly potent, the potential for harm is greater than it was a few years ago. As a result of hybrid seeds, and the wider availability of domestically produced marijuana, which is stronger than the imported product, the marijuana used by most Americans contains three times as much of the active agent called THC than it did ten years ago.

Likewise, the cocaine that is sold today is purer and thus more likely to lead to overdose, respiratory failure, and cardiac arrest. Whether in the hands of casual or frequent users, cocaine can be lethal. This is particularly true of crack, a smokable form of cocaine that produces a more euphoric high and is more addictive than cocaine that is snorted. When crack first appeared in the mid-1980s, it quickly became the preferred drug for many users and it signaled a new stage in the epidemic.

Recently, officials of the federal Drug Enforcement Administration have expressed concern about another

DRUG THREATS TO AMERICA

DO SOMETHING! ANYTHING!!

YUPPIES ON COCAINE

POOR PEOPLE ON CRACK

JUNKIES ON HEROIN

POLITICIANS ON DRUG HYSTERIA

BEN SARGENT, AUSTIN AMERICAN-STATESMAN

illicit substance, "speed," or metham-phetamine. A growing number of clandestine labs on the West Coast are manufacturing this powerful stimulant, which is often called "poor man's cocaine." Cheaper than cocaine, speed is available as a powder that can be snorted, injected, or swallowed. Unlike cocaine, it does not have to be grown abroad and smuggled into the United States. In makeshift labs, chemicals that are readily available and relatively cheap are used to produce metham-phetamine, whose street value per pound is more than $30,000. According to DEA official Ron D'Ulisse, making speed is "easier than a Betty Crocker cake." As speed appears in drug markets across the country, the National Institute on Drug Abuse warns, "Domestically produced methamphetamine looms as a poten-tial national drug crisis for the 1990s."

OUT OF CONTROL

By 1988, lawmakers and the Ameri-can public shared the perception that the drug problem is getting worse and that federal anti-drug efforts seem to be ineffective in stemming the tide. Introducing congressional hearings on national drug strategy in April 1988, Representative Benjamin Gilman remarked that "America's drug problem has continued to worsen. . . . Illegal narcotics are in our cities and suburbs, in our schools and in our streets. . . . Internationally, the picture is also bleak. The power, greed, and ruthlessness of the drug cartels continues to grow. If we do not check drug trafficking and drug abuse, the very foundation of our society will be threatened. It is time, past time actually, that this country formulated and enacted an effective national strategy to combat drugs."

Polls show that most Americans share that assessment. More than four

out of five people agree that the illegal drug problem is out of control. By the same margin, an ABC poll taken in September 1988 showed that most Americans think illegal drugs are a bigger problem today than they were five years ago.

The message of one poll after another is that there is strong support for tough responses to the drug problem, including use of the military to stop drugs before they get to the U.S. border. A 1988 *Washington Post* survey found that a large majority supports such measures as allowing police to stop cars at random to search for drugs. Half said they favor manda-tory one-year jail sentences for cocaine users, even first-time offenders. A third of the respondents said that police should be permitted to search homes without a court order "even if the houses of people like you are some-times searched by mistake."

Urged on by public pressure, few members of Congress were willing to risk the accusation that they are soft on drugs. Legislators acknowledged the importance of coming up with something more effective than current anti-drug measures. "A public relations campaign is not sufficient," said Representative Tony Coelho of California. "People want results."

At the same time, there was growing concern among legislators that some of the proposed initiatives on drugs are mindlessly tough measures that appeal to the public but are likely to do little to solve the problem. In the words of Senator Dale Bumpers, "Just to grow hair on your chest here on the Senate floor so you can . . . tell everyone how tough you are on drugs is no solution."

Columnists speculated that tough talk about drugs might amount to nothing more than an election-year diversion. "Tough talk about drugs,"

WHAT'S FOR SALE IN THE DRUG MARKET

To follow the drug debate, it helps to know something about which drugs are available — their names, their effects, and the degree of danger associated with their use. Most illicit drugs belong to one of these five categories:

STIMULANTS

Amphetamines (commonly called, "speed," "uppers," or "whites") are synthetic drugs generally made in U.S. laboratories. The effects of speed resemble adrenaline, the body's natural stimulant. A single dose stimulates the body for four hours or more, often precluding sleeping or eating. Continued use of speed eventually wears out the body, causing hardening of the arteries and palpitations.

Cocaine comes from the leaves of the coca plant. Available in the form of a white powder, it is generally taken by snorting through the nostrils. Cocaine produces an intense "high" that is followed by an equally intense "low." In high doses, cocaine can cause death by disrupting the brain's control of the heart and respiration.

Crack ("rock") is a concentrated form of cocaine that has been available over the past few years. Because pellets of crack are smoked, it is quickly absorbed into the blood stream, producing an extreme sense of euphoria. Crack is highly addictive and very dangerous.

MDMA ("ecstacy") is a synthetic drug that combines amphetamines with synthetic mescaline to produce a mildly hallucinogenic stimulant. Ecstacy has also been shown to destroy nerve endings in that part of the brain which regulates sleep, mood, sexual arousal, perception of pain, and aggressive behavior. Medical experts claim that regular use can cause paranoia and psychosis.

DEPRESSANTS

Barbiturates (also known as "downers," "reds," or Seconals) are sedative-hypnotic drugs. When used in larger doses, barbiturates can cause both physical and psychological dependence. Over time, barbiturate use increases anxiety and depression. Barbiturate overdoses are a particular hazard. High doses shut down the brain's control centers, leading to death from lack of oxygen.

Heroin is a narcotic derived from the opium poppy plant that, in proper doses, relieves pain. In high doses, especially when injected, heroin produces a feeling of euphoria. As tolerance to heroin develops, many users become addicted. An overdose can cause death by stopping respiration.

PCP

Phencyclidine ("angel dust") is a synthetic compound. It was invented in the 1950s as a surgical anesthetic, but was withdrawn from the market after patients reported bizarre reactions. Subsequently, PCP reappeared on the black market. In powdered form, PCP is usually smoked. It stimulates the body in certain ways and depresses it in others. PCP interrupts those parts of the brain that control intellect and keep instincts in check. Users often experience a sense of confusion, agitation, and paranoia, and they are prone to violent behavior.

MARIJUANA

Marijuana (also called "smoke," "pot," or "grass") consists of the crumbled leaves and flowering tops of the cannabis plant rolled into cigarettes or "joints." For many users, marijuana also acts as a mild hallucinogen, causing certain distortions in perception. Marijuana is not as powerful or as toxic as other illicit drugs. While it does have a potential for creating psychological dependence, it is not physically addictive. Long-term negative effects of regular marijuana use remain a topic of heated debate.

Hashish ("hash") contains a higher concentration of THC than marijuana and is thus a more potent drug. It is sold in solid chunks and usually smoked in pipes.

HALLUCINOGENS

LSD ("acid") is a synthetic drug not found in nature. Taken orally, LSD causes a "trip" which lasts for 10-12 hours. Like other hallucinogens, its effects differ among users depending on the setting in which it is taken. LSD causes perceptual changes, particularly increased awareness of sounds, colors, and textures. While LSD is not addictive, its effects are unpleasant and disorienting for some users. As with marijuana, debate continues about long-term dangers that may be associated with use of hallucinogens.

wrote columnist George Will, "may be the opiate of the masses this election year. It beats talk about the deficit, and politicians love it because everyone agrees about the objective — less drug abuse. Politicians stand four-square against sin, starting with drugs. But righteous indignation can become an addiction that saps society's reasonableness."

Most people agree about the objective of the anti-drug campaign. The dispute is over strategies, not objectives. What is likely to prove successful in stopping drugs? Which measures are compatible with the other things we value — such as civil liberties, the freedom to do what we choose except when individual behavior harms others or creates a public menace? Which measures are likely to be effective and which are simply unworkable?

As Congress moved toward a final version of the comprehensive drug bill, commentators warned about the danger of overreacting to the public's call for tough new measures. "Under the pressures of an election year and a public in near-hysteria over the drug problem," wrote columnist Tom Wicker, "Congress has been debating some horrendously punitive, in many cases irrelevant, 'remedies.' "

President Reagan's Commission on Organized Crime recommended a nationwide program of drug testing to apply to all federal employees, as well as employees working for private firms awarded government contracts. In addition, the commission urged other private employers to initiate similar programs. Judging by recent polls, a majority supports mandatory drug testing in the workplace, even though only 5 percent say drug use at their jobs is a big problem. The question, both for lawmakers and for the public, is whether a program of mandatory testing is good public policy.

Similar questions were raised about an anti-drug measure supported by many members of the House that would expand the use of illegally seized evidence. Members of Congress also engaged in last-minute discussion about whether the law should permit the execution of "drug kingpins," big-time traffickers who commit or order murders of law enforcement officials. To its critics, that measure typifies the worst kind of drug policy, one that appeals to bloodthirsty attitudes but is unlikely to deter the drug trade.

ANTI-DRUG ABUSE ACT

Finally, after repeated sessions in which congressional leaders met to iron out differences between the House and Senate bills, the 100th Congress passed an anti-drug bill as its final act. The most important feature of the Anti-Drug Abuse Act of 1988 is that it shifts the emphasis of the war on drugs from law enforcement to education, rehabilitation, and other efforts to reduce demand. While more than 70 percent of previous federal efforts had been devoted to enforcement and interdiction, the new law specifies that the government shall provide equal funding for prevention and treatment programs.

In response to demands for tough measures to stop traffickers and users, the law provides additional funds for stepped-up border control and international narcotics control. It permits the death penalty for drug kingpins and anyone convicted of drug-related killings and it provides stiffer penalties for convicted drug traffickers. One of the law's controversial features is that it imposes stiff fines of up to $10,000 for the possession of even small amounts of illegal drugs. It also allows the government to withdraw certain

DRUGS AND CRIME

■ In selected cities, percentage of men arrested on any charge who tested positive for any drugs, excluding marijuana

■ Percentage of men arrested who tested positive for cocaine

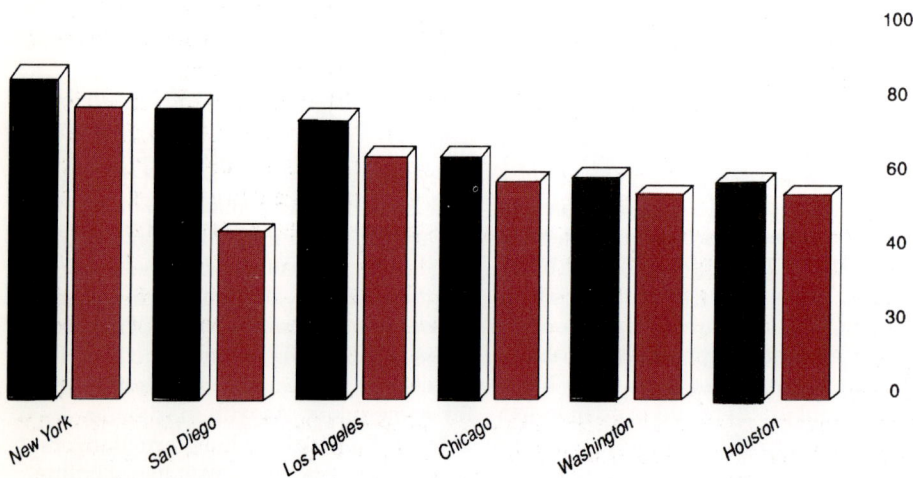

New York   San Diego   Los Angeles   Chicago   Washington   Houston

Note: Study conducted April through June 1988
Source: National Institute of Justice

"America's drug problem has continued to worsen. It is time that this society formulated and enacted an effective national strategy to combat drugs."

— Representative Benjamin Gilman

federal benefits from individuals convicted of drug possession or use.

Along with other members of Congress, Senate Democratic leader Robert C. Byrd praised the new law, calling it "the most comprehensive and strong" drug legislation ever passed. Referring to its emphasis on reducing demand as well as supply, many people applauded the new law as a prudent combination of strategies.

However, critics pointed out that in an election-year fervor to produce the new law, members of Congress had little time to consider which approach to drug control makes the most sense. Because the new law tries to move in several directions at once, it may accomplish very little. "This bill brings us no closer to a coherent strategy in the war on drugs," said a *New Republic* editorial. "U.S. drug policy continues to consist of several distinct components that, to the extent they're connected at all, are connected by contradictions."

DRUG POLICY

The Anti-Drug Abuse Act goes into effect on September 1, 1989, when William Bennett, the new "drug czar," will be responsible for coordinating the government's war on narcotics. The passage of the law and the installation of a "drug czar" raise basic questions about how to stem the tide of illicit drug use. What should the priorities of an anti-drug policy be? Should most of the government's resources be invested in trying to stop drugs before they reach our shores? Or should most public resources be invested in efforts to reduce the sale and use of illicit substances?

In recent years, much of the discussion about drug policy has taken place

between proponents of these approaches. But some people conclude, in the words of a *New Republic* editorial, that "in the war on drugs, virtually nothing demonstrably works in an acceptable fashion." If this is true, it makes little sense to pour more resources into such efforts.

Essentially, four strategies have been proposed to deal with the drug crisis, and these four approaches frame our discussion:

American Roulette

BRIAN DUFFY, *DES MOINES REGISTER*

Choice #1 is based on the conviction that the most promising way to deal with the drug problem is to stop drugs at their source — primarily in Third World countries where coca leaves, opium poppy plants, and marijuana are grown. Advocates of this strategy favor stepped-up eradication efforts, more effective interdiction efforts to stop drug smugglers, and expanded involvement of the military in the battle against drugs.

Choice #2 focuses on domestic law enforcement, stopping the drug problem by targeting domestic dealers — both wholesalers and street-corner drug dealers. Proponents of this position are convinced that efforts to identify, prosecute, and imprison drug dealers must be expanded.

Choice #3 focuses on the demand for drugs rather than the supply. Advocates of this strategy favor a variety of measures designed to discourage people from using drugs, ranging from education and treatment to punitive measures targeted at users, even individuals who only occasionally use drugs. Those measures include arrest, fines, seizure of property, forfeiture of drivers' licenses and other privileges.

Choice #4 represents a different approach to the problem. Exasperated by the seemingly endless crime and corruption generated by the illicit drug trade, many people want to control the situation by legalizing at least some drugs and regulating their sale. From this perspective, drug use is unlikely to be eliminated entirely. But by making drugs legal, we can at least cut down on drug-related crime.

Although each choice leads to a distinctive course of action, these strategies are not mutually exclusive. Some combination of these strategies may be the best way to control the use of drugs in America. Different strategies may be appropriate for different drugs or for different communities.

In any case, public debate about these alternatives is essential if we are to move toward a consensus about how to deal with what is widely regarded as the nation's most pressing domestic issue.■

CHOICE #1
STEPPING UP THE
INTERNATIONAL DRUG WAR

"The most promising way to cope with the drug crisis is to destroy drugs at their source or in transit, before they get to the U.S. distribution network."

The international narcotics trade, the world's most profitable industry, is the source of roughly 80 percent of the illicit drugs used in the United States. Drugs come from all over the world: from Colombia, Peru, Belize, Mexico, Pakistan, Afghanistan, and Thailand, among other nations. Each year, traffickers smuggle into the United States some 5 metric tons of heroin, more than 100 metric tons of cocaine, and an estimated 5,000 metric tons of marijuana.

Responding to America's appetite for illicit substances, Latin American drug merchants have expanded their scope and refined their brutal tactics to dominate the international drug trade. Although Mexico remains the largest exporter of heroin and marijuana to the United States, cocaine is now the hemisphere's most lucrative drug. Colombians are responsible for shipping 80 percent of the world's cocaine.

In Colombia, cocaine production is the mainstay of the nation's economy, surpassing the production of coffee. The Colombian drug cartel, which has operated for about a decade, has become a multinational organization with private armies, close ties to political and criminal leaders in a dozen nations, and vast financial resources.

Leaders of the cartel rely on a policy of greed and fear — as the Colombians call it, *plomo o plata*, lead or silver. In other words, take the money or take the bullet. Lubricated by payments to public officials estimated to be more than $100 million a year, the influence of the Colombian *narcotraficantes* extends from rank-and-file police officers to heads of state.

With the tacit cooperation of Colombian judges, narcotics peddlers are rarely convicted, and when convicted rarely serve long sentences. With the assistance of customs and immigration officials in neighboring nations, members of the Colombian drug cartel set up processing laboratories and landing strips, and launder billions of dollars in illicit profits.

Increasingly brazen, members of the drug cartel have shown that they will resort to any means to protect their illicit business. Several years ago, the Reagan administration pushed for a tough extradition treaty to stop the drug trade by putting Colombian drug kingpins in U.S. prisons. Declaring "total war" on anyone who favors extradition, the cartel responded with a brutal campaign of intimidation. As evidence of their insistence that the 1986 extradition treaty between the United States and Colombia be declared unconstitutional, Attorney General Hoyos was assassinated along with Colombia's Justice Minister, a leading newspaper editor, a senior police officer, 26 judges, as well as other prominent citizens who defended extradition to break the power of the drug cartel. Finally, the country's Supreme Court ruled against the treaty. Subsequently, arrest warrants against all but a few traffickers were revoked.

As Colombian prosecutor Francisco Bernal Castillo recently put it, as a result of the drug thugs "our way of life is being threatened." The drug trade also threatens their form of government. As in other Latin American countries where drug enforcement efforts put enormous pressure on fledgling liberal institutions, the political institutions of this nation are being destroyed by corruption and violence.

The success of the Colombian cartel illustrates the extraordinary influence of the international drug merchants who resort to any means to continue trafficking in cocaine, the substance that is most responsible for America's worsening drug crisis.

OUTMANNED AND OUTGUNNED

According to a 1988 U. S. State Department report on international narcotics, the Colombian cocaine industry shows no signs of slowing down. Some 23 countries have joined the United States in eradicating drug crops, which led to the destruction of large amounts of coca leaf as well as opium and marijuana. Nonetheless, the Colombian cocaine industry is growing. Compared to 1983 figures, the State Department estimates that twice as much coca is now cultivated.

The State Department reports that production of coca, marijuana, and opium-poppy crops in drug-producing nations has grown substantially over the past year. In the words of a recent State Department report, "Corruption of government officials, bribery, trafficker intimidation and violence, and the stark fact that governments are outmanned, outgunned, and outspent by narcotics traffickers continue to undermine global efforts to stop narcotics production and trafficking."

Most Americans regard the international drug trade as the chief threat to the nation's security. According to a 1988 *New York Times*/CBS poll, by a margin of 3-to-1, Americans are convinced that fighting the flow of drugs into this country is more important than fighting communism. The nation is under attack by ruthless and well-financed drug lords, conclude proponents

of this first choice, and we appear to be losing the war.

In the words of Brooklyn District Attorney Elizabeth Holzman and Representative Stephen Solarz, "With ample resources and a strategy of eradication and interdiction, the cocaine industry of Latin America could be brought to its knees. We are losing the war on drugs because our government has not taken the initiative to provide the ammunition or a battle plan for victory. Fighting the cocaine cartel will cost money, but the price tag is far cheaper than the continued high costs associated with drug abuse."

DRUG-PRODUCING NATIONS

From this perspective, the most promising way to cope with the drug crisis is to destroy narcotics at their source or in transit, before they get to the U.S. distribution network. If drugs are to be destroyed at their source, drug-producing nations need help from the U.S. government with eradication efforts and other enforcement activities, including the destruction of clandestine labs and airfields. Drug-producing nations also need help in strengthening their legal

JIM MORIN, *THE MIAMI HERALD*

and judicial systems to eliminate narcotics organizations.

In recent years, the U.S. government has supported activities intended to eradicate coca, opium, and marijuana in 15 countries. Currently, the United States supports eradication by providing chemical herbicides to producer countries as well as specialized equipment such as aircraft equipped for aerial spraying. U.S. military advisers help to train law enforcement officials in Bolivia, Colombia, and Peru for helicopter raids on processing plants. In 1987, Bolivian police, assisted by U.S. drug agents, raided and destroyed a jungle laboratory that produced cocaine which authorities said had a street value of almost $10 million a day. Another U.S.-assisted operation in that country resulted in the destruction of 3,000 acres of coca plants.

Since it is easier to destroy crops in the field than to locate processed drugs on smuggling routes or on the streets in the United States, proponents of this approach are convinced that reducing the foreign supply is the most promising way to reduce drug use in the United States.

However, there are substantial impediments to successful crop reduction. In more than a dozen nations, the production of narcotics is a mainstay of the local economy. Farmers usually do not have a readily available alternative crop or one that is so profitable. In Burma and Thailand, for example, opium poppy is the only crop that can be raised successfully in some areas.

Replacing the income farmers lose when they abandon production of narcotics is essential to the success of such efforts. Currently, the U. S. Agency for International Development spends $25 million a year to provide alternative income for farmers who no longer cultivate illicit narcotic crops.

If such efforts are aggressively pursued, drug-producing nations will need far more assistance from the United States — both technical assistance and foreign aid. In a 1988 report on drug trafficking, the U.S. State Department advocated providing as much as $300 million in additional American assistance to drug-producing nations.

Some people are convinced that a massive foreign aid effort — a mini-Marshall Plan — is the only realistic way to persuade nations to curb their drug production. The objective of such a plan would be to encourage the cultivation of other marketable crops and to promote economic development. An ambitious effort along these lines would require aid far in excess of that currently offered to nations such as Colombia, Mexico, Pakistan, and Burma.

CARROTS AND STICKS

Advocates of this choice are convinced that while the U.S. government offers the carrot of increased assistance to drug-producing nations, it should also use the stick of sanctions against nations that do not cooperate. Confronted with an influx of drugs from overseas, the United States should get tough with nations that tolerate the drug industry as well as nations that collaborate with drug traffickers.

The 1986 anti-drug law requires the President to certify annually that 25 countries identified as drug producers or drug-transit nations are cooperating with efforts to crack down on the illicit trade. The law specifies that nations risk losing half of their economic and military aid and could suffer other penalties such as trade restrictions. The sanctions can be waived only if the President decides that overriding

THIS IS A DEAD AMERICAN TEEN-AGE DRUG USER.

THIS IS THE DRUG DEALER WHO SOLD THE DRUGS TO THE DEAD TEEN-AGE DRUG USER.

THIS IS THE SUPPLIER WHO SOLD THE DRUGS TO THE DEALER WHO SOLD THEM TO THE DEAD TEEN-AGE DRUG USER.

THIS IS THE DRUG LORD WHO SOLD THE DRUGS TO THE SUPPLIER WHO SOLD TO THE DEALER WHO SOLD TO THE DEAD TEEN-AGE DRUG USER.

THIS IS THE U.S.-BACKED MILITARY DICTATOR WHO ACCOMMODATED THE DRUG LORD WHO ETC. ETC....

GO, CONTRAS

NORIEGA

PANAMA

THIS IS A DEAD AMERICAN TEEN-AGE DRUG USER.

JIM MORIN, *THE MIAMI HERALD*

> *"While the U.S. government should use the carrot of increased assistance to nations that halt drug production and trafficking, it should also use the stick of sanctions against governments that do not cooperate."*

THE WORLDWIDE DRUG TRADE

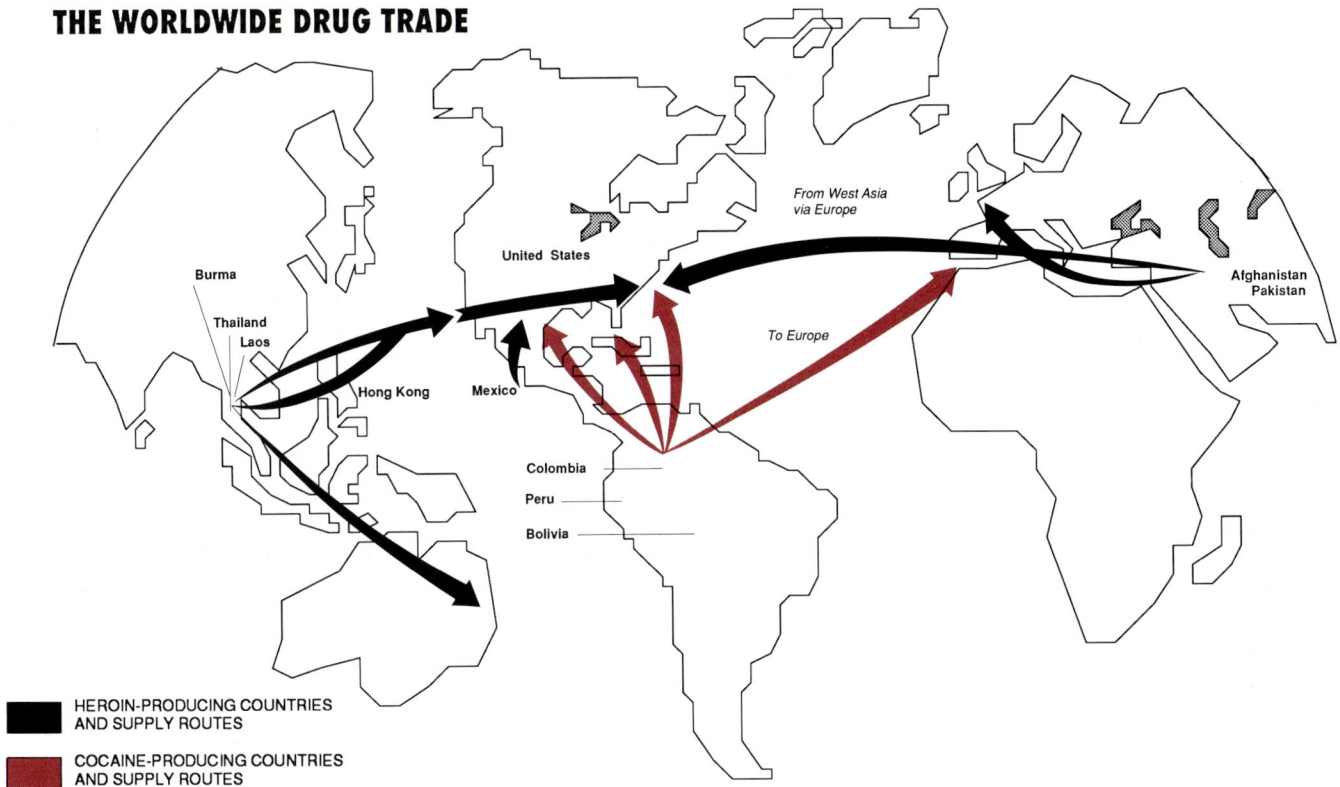

HEROIN-PRODUCING COUNTRIES AND SUPPLY ROUTES

COCAINE-PRODUCING COUNTRIES AND SUPPLY ROUTES

national interests are at stake.

However, since it was written into law in 1986 the decertification process has not been used to penalize an American ally. Seventeen drug-producing and transiting nations, including Mexico and Colombia, have been faulted for their failure to extradite drug dealers to the United States and for not destroying cocaine labs. Nonetheless, they have been certified and continue to receive U.S. aid and assistance. In each case, the Administration argued that the drug issue should be subordinated to other American interests, ranging from support for insurgents fighting leftist regimes to the belief that punishing drug-producing nations might destabilize them and thwart U.S. security efforts.

Advocates of this first choice believe that the sanctions provided by the decertification process *must* be em-ployed. The United States should not operate on a business-as-usual basis with nations that permit drug production, trafficking, or laundering of drug profits. "You have to balance priorities," says Francis J. McNeil, a former Deputy Assistant Secretary of State. "But the fact is that we have not balanced priorities. We have always put narcotics at the bottom of the totem pole."

BORDER PATROL

If narcotics cannot be eradicated at their source, traffickers can be apprehended as they attempt to smuggle drugs across the border. By some measures, America's interdiction policy has been successful. In 1986, for example, 27 tons of refined cocaine were seized at the border — 16 times more than in 1981. Clearly, smuggling is getting riskier.

But no one claims that drug interdiction efforts are successful in intercept-ing more than a small fraction of the narcotics that are brought across the border. The United States is the world's largest trading nation, which means that huge amounts of imported products flow into the country daily through thousands of sea, air, and land entry points. Few people are prepared to take the measures necessary to monitor each of those entry points and to inspect virtually every package that enters the country.

One measure that has been repeatedly proposed is wider use of the military in drug interdiction efforts. In the words of New York Mayor Ed Koch: "The massive illicit drug trade can be stopped only by the direct involvement of our armed forces.... You can't win a war without weapons. Until the weapons are committed, the drug invaders will have a virtual free pass across our borders."

For several years, the Pentagon has played a limited role in drug interdiction efforts. In 1987, for example, U.S. aircraft ranging from reconnaissance planes to B-52 bombers flew some 16,000 hours of surveillance near American borders, and Coast Guard "bust" teams spent 2,500 days aboard U.S. Navy ships. In the same year, the Pentagon spent $91 million on drug enforcement and loaned millions of dollars worth of equipment to law enforcement agencies for this purpose.

Still, the principal mission of the U.S. military is combat readiness, not fighting the war on drugs. In fact, the military is prohibited by law from getting involved in domestic law enforcement. Nonetheless, in June 1988, the Armed Services Committees of the House and Senate advocated expanded involvement of the military in the war against drugs. They argued that only the U.S. military has the resources and equipment to rival the sophisticated equipment used by international merchants to smuggle narcotics into the United States.

Testifying on behalf of the U.S. Conference of Mayors in June 1988, Mayor Donna Owens of Toledo, Ohio, said: "America has been invaded by an enemy as cruel and powerful as any foreign enemy we have faced, and there is no demilitarized zone. The Constitution says that Congress should provide for the common defense, and we must defend our borders against this drug invasion."

Proponents of this first response to the drug crisis are convinced that new measures should be taken to step up the war on drugs, to eradicate narcotics at their source, and to counter the influence of international drug merchants.

ED GAMBLE, *THE FLORIDA TIMES - UNION*

WHAT CRITICS SAY

Advocates of a stepped-up war on international drug dealers conclude that the reason efforts along these lines have not been successful is that they have not been aggressively pursued. In the words of Representative Charles Rangel, chairman of the House Select Committee on Narcotics Abuse and Control, "The administration has refused to provide either the money or the leadership to fight a real war on drugs."

To others, however, repeated assertions of the need for a more aggressive war on drugs recall futile efforts to escalate the war in Southeast Asia. As policy analyst David Boas remarks, "Today, we're waist-deep in another unwinnable war and many political leaders want to push on. This time, it's a war on drugs. As in the case of Vietnam — and Prohibition, another unwinnable war — many politicians can't stand losing a war. Instead of acknowledging failure, they want to escalate."

The best measure of the effectiveness of anti-drug efforts, say critics of a more aggressive war on drugs, is not the amount of narcotics seized by enforcement officials but the supply available to American users and its price. The amount of cocaine seized has increased dramatically — from 2 tons in 1981 to almost 30 tons in 1987. Yet the street price of cocaine *declined* from $125 a gram in 1983 to $80 a gram in 1987.

No matter how many drugs are confiscated, even more are smuggled into the country. Increasingly, law enforcement officials have come to agree with Senator Dale Bumpers, who concludes that "There isn't any way to keep drugs out of this country."

AMERICA'S INFLUENCE ABROAD

Critics have reservations about whether anti-drug efforts should be the chief consideration in our relations with Latin American nations and drug-producing nations in other regions. They recall what happened when the Reagan administration sent American troops to Bolivia to assist that country's anti-drug efforts. Despite massive preparations, the effort was disappointing. While 80-100

> **"America has been invaded by an enemy as cruel and powerful as any foreign enemy we have faced. Congress should provide for the common defense. And we must defend our borders against this drug invasion."**
>
> — Mayor Donna Owens, Toledo, Ohio

such labs were believed to be located in the region, the raids uncovered just 2 of them. Not a single major drug trafficker was captured.

To critics of this approach, the Bolivian example illustrates why U.S. efforts to eradicate drugs at their source have been only modestly successful. With American assistance, the Bolivian government offered farmers an incentive of $2,000 for every hectare — roughly 2.5 acres — of coca they eliminated. Even accompanied by cash incentives, the effort faced strong opposition.

In Bolivia, as elsewhere, when local governments pursue anti-drug efforts they face opposition not only from drug trafficking groups but also from coca-growing farmers. Praised in the United States as a model of what governments in drug-producing nations can do with American assistance, the Bolivian effort wiped out just 3 percent of the country's coca crop and stimulated planting elsewhere.

While American foreign policy promotes political and economic stability in developing nations, aggressive anti-drug policies often have a destabilizing effect. U.S. allies are often annoyed at America's anti-drug obsession, especially when American officials tell other nations what to do.

Following a 1978 helicopter tour of the Guajira Peninsula in 1978, DEA Administrator Peter Bensinger characterized Colombia's marijuana industry as a "national security threat" and urged the military to occupy the region. His words triggered a storm of protest, including a reply from Colombian official Guillermo Linares who characterized his suggestion as "imprudent interference in the affairs of this country. Neither he nor other foreign officials should tell the Colombian government what to do — much

less what our armed forces should do."

Many people are concerned that sanctions against governments in drug-producing nations antagonize our allies. In a deeper sense, those efforts put the burden for solving a drug crisis, fueled by American demand, on Third World nations.

THE MILITARY SOLUTION

Impatient with the lack of success in previous anti-drug initiatives, members of Congress have on several occasions proposed increased military involvement in the war on drugs. In 1986, for example, the House of Representatives passed a measure to expand the role of the armed forces, who were instructed to "seal the borders" within 45 days of the passage of the act.

Critics ridiculed the proposal. Senator Sam Nunn, head of the Armed Services Committee, argued that it was "the equivalent of passing a law saying

that the President shall, by Thanksgiving, devise a cure for the common cold." The measure, said Nunn, would require deploying the entire U.S. Navy to American waters.

By and large, critics of this strategy agree that drug enforcement is a task for law enforcement officials, not a military mission. The war on drugs is an unconventional war that the military is ill equipped to fight. Military involvement in the anti-drug effort detracts from the principal mission of the armed forces.

Officials of the U.S. Customs Service and the Drug Enforcement Administration have repeatedly said that proposals to involve the military in the war on drugs reflect a lack of understanding about how drug smugglers operate. Heroin and cocaine are often smuggled into this country on ships, where drugs are hidden in commercial cargo ranging from frozen fruit pulp from Ecuador to furniture from Brazil. Of the 7 million cargo containers that

One of the Coast Guard's functions is to identify drugs seized at the U.S. border.

Paraphernalia used for smoking crack, a potent and popular form of cocaine

UPI/BETTMAN NEWSPHOTOS

enter the country every year, the Customs Service is able to inspect only 3 percent. "I don't know of anything the military can do to help us in this area," says Customs Agent Patrick O'Brien. "We've given a lot of thought to the container problem. The only way to stop it is to get on the forklifts and open up all the boxes."

Beyond such practical reservations, critics of military involvement in the anti-drug effort raise a more basic objection. "Are we still a republic with a limited government and a civilian-controlled military whose sole purpose is to defend this country against attack?" asks writer Bill Kaufman, "or are we to become a huge Banana Republic, where a jack-booted military acts to secure social control at home and hemispheric hegemony abroad?"

PUSH DOWN, POP UP

Critics are no more optimistic about stepped-up eradication or interdiction efforts. As sensible as it seems to tackle the drug problem at its source, the narcotics trade is a hydra-headed monster. Drug experts call it the "push-down, pop-up" phenomenon. No matter how successful drug enforcement officials are in suppressing or eliminating one international supplier, another steps in to fill the demand. Several years ago, when the herbicide paraquat was sprayed on Mexican marijuana fields, it virtually eliminated that country as a seller to the U.S. market. But the supply was only temporarily interrupted because Colombian producers quickly filled the void.

Similarly, no matter how ingenious law enforcement officials are in shutting down smuggling routes, drug merchants find other ways to get drugs across the border. That explains

why the authors of a study of the drug trade conducted by the Rand Corporation concluded that "the basic point is that the supply of drugs can never be eliminated." The study suggests that it would be extremely difficult to reduce drug consumption in this country by even 5 percent through more stringent interdiction efforts.

In the words of drug expert John Kaplan, "The ingenuity of smugglers, the tremendous volume of legitimate trade, and the huge number of individuals crossing our borders make it impracticable to achieve the kind of increases in the interdiction rate that would make heroin and cocaine significantly less available or more expensive in the United States."

In the unlikely event that smugglers could be prevented from bringing drugs across the borders, domestic producers would meet the demand for drugs, either by cultivating the same drugs (such as marijuana) that are currently imported, or by producing synthetic substitutes (such as methamphetamine).

As Peter Reuter, author of the Rand study concludes, "The notion of production control is appealing. If we apply enough of the Band Aids such as interdiction, we shall strike at the fundamental problem, drug production itself. Unfortunately, there is plenty of evidence that U.S. foreign drug control efforts have been unsuccessful. The failures are not a result of incompetence or inadequate resources. They are inherent in this approach to the problem."

If critics of stepped-up efforts to control international drug merchants don't regard this as a promising strategy, there is another way to choke off the supply. We could step up law enforcement efforts to stop narcotics after they enter the United States. This is the essence of a second strategy in the war on drugs. ∎

CHOICE #2
CRACKING DOWN ON DEALERS: THE ENFORCEMENT STRATEGY

"Law enforcement officials are overwhelmed by an army of drug dealers. Efforts to identify, prosecute, and imprison drug dealers must be expanded."

In December 1988, 150 heavily armed New York City police officers, federal marshals, and DEA agents raided three buildings in upper Manhattan, arresting drug dealers who used the buildings to sell cocaine and crack. Local residents cheered the effort to reclaim a neighborhood that had been taken over by drug dealers.

The action was the latest in a series of moves by New York City law enforcement officials to target places where drugs are sold as well as the people who sell them. Recalling that a police officer recently had been shot by a suspected crack dealer just three blocks away, Mayor Koch and Police Commissioner Benjamin Ward said that the raid was intended to show drug dealers that they are not invincible. They vowed to keep up the pressure on narcotics traffickers.

The raid in upper Manhattan illustrates an approach that many people regard as the most promising way to deal with the drug crisis.

Proponents of this second course of action are convinced that efforts to arrest, prosecute, and imprison drug dealers must be expanded. After all, the law specifies that drugs are illegal, and provides specific punishments for anyone who violates these laws.

Yet in many cities street-corner drug sales are readily apparent, which encourages disrespect for the law and permits individuals to buy virtually any illicit substance they want. In many regions of the country, law enforcement officials seem to be overwhelmed by drug dealers who are bolder, more visible, and more solidly entrenched than ever before.

DRUGS FOR SALE

The situation was bad enough several years ago in places like Los Angeles when violent gangs, such as the Bloods and the Crips, began to dominate the local market for crack and cocaine. Since then, the Bloods, Crips, and other gangs have spread to cities unaccustomed to drugs and drug-related violence and the drug

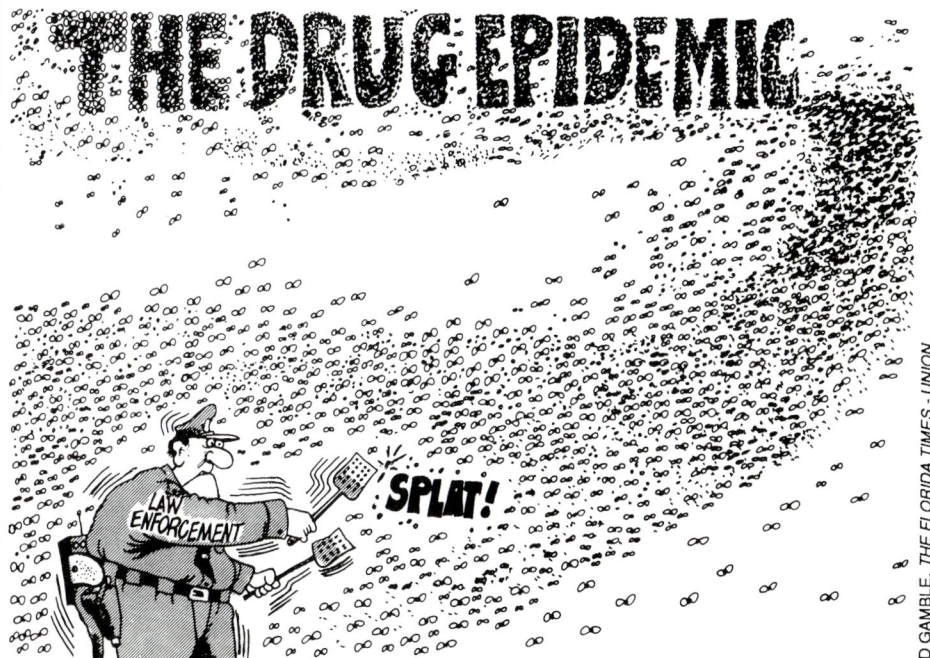

THE DRUG EPIDEMIC

SPLAT!

LAW ENFORCEMENT

ED GAMBLE, *THE FLORIDA TIMES - UNION*

problem has become worse.

In 1987, Los Angeles gangs began moving up the coast to Portland, Seattle, and Anchorage. More recently, they have moved east, setting up operations in several cities in the Midwest. Heavily armed, the drug dealers intimidate the opposition and undersell the competition. Federal drug officials report that in each city where they set up shop the level of violence increases along with the number of arms seized in arrests. In each instance, the level of crack use rises soon after the gangs arrive.

Omaha is one of the cities where West Coast gangs have set up an outpost. "We really didn't have a crack problem here until this year," said FBI Agent John Pakonin in 1988, "but now the stuff is easy to get." As Robert Armstrong, director of the Omaha Housing Authority reports, drugs are readily available. "These dealers have no fear. Whether they are Crips or Crip imitators, they sell their drugs anytime they feel like selling. And they intimidate people. They make them afraid to call the police by letting them know they have guns."

In Detroit, the crack market was dominated until recently by a ruthlessly efficient outfit called the Chambers Brothers Organization. Before federal agents apprehended its leaders in 1988, the operation's daily sales were estimated to be in excess of $1 million. According to accounts of drug agents, the Detroit organization, which had hundreds of employees, was run like a Fortune 500 firm. To lure buyers to crack, the operation used marketing techniques such as discount coupons and two-for-one sales.

If drugs are most often sold and used by youths in the inner cities, this is a problem in most communities, and not just among young people. In Columbia, South Carolina, police charged the operator of an ice cream parlor with selling cocaine from Mr. Yummy trucks. In Houston, a 74-year-old grandmother was convicted of dealing

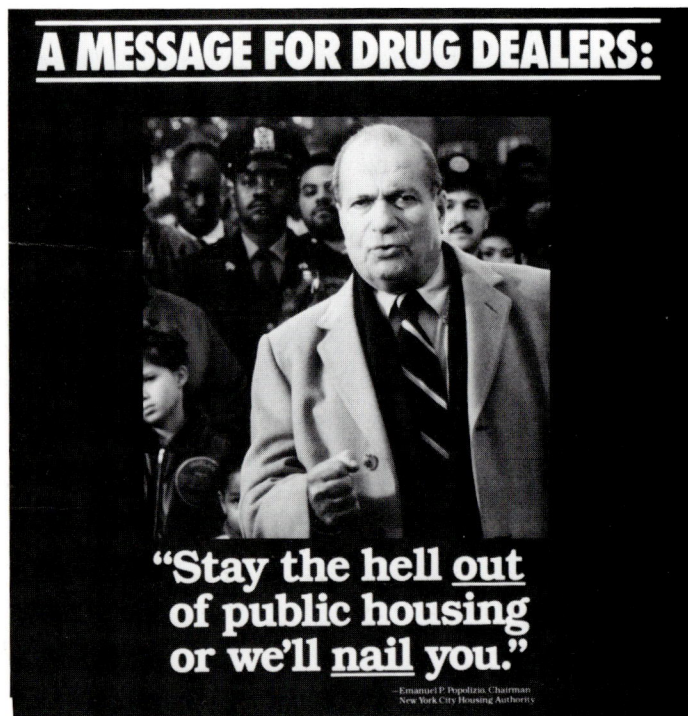

A MESSAGE FOR DRUG DEALERS:

"Stay the hell **out** of public housing or we'll **nail** you."

—Emanuel P. Popolizio, Chairman
New York City Housing Authority

COURTESY: NARCOTICS TASK FORCE, NYC HOUSING AUTHORITY

Valium and marijuana from her home. In Philadelphia, a dentist pleaded guilty to selling millions of dollars worth of cocaine each month to stockbrokers and lawyers in a scheme which local newspapers dubbed the "Yuppie cocaine ring."

A nationwide poll conducted by the *Washington Post* in March 1988, found that one in three Americans knows of a place within a mile of their home where drugs can be purchased. In the words of a Drug Enforcement Administration official, "in many middle-class communities buying drugs is like buying Tupperware."

VIGOROUS ENFORCEMENT

To proponents of this second approach to the problem, the fact that drugs can be bought and sold with impunity is the clearest indication that we are losing the war. One of the basic tasks of government, as stated in the Constitution, is to ensure domestic tranquillity — which means, among other things, preserving law and order, protecting citizens against criminal acts and violent behavior. Yet drug dealers have literally taken over the streets in many communities. Even where the presence of dealers is not readily apparent, use of illicit drugs leads to increased muggings and burglaries and to other socially disruptive behavior. Advocates of this second choice conclude that law enforcement officials must act more forcefully to apprehend and punish drug dealers.

Police in many communities already devote a significant portion of their time and resources to enforcing the drug laws and dealing with drug-related violence. In a 1988 survey conducted by the *National Law Journal*, when prosecutors across the country were asked how much time they devote to drug-related crime, 53 percent said that drug-related cases amount to 10 to 25 per-

"The choice is clear: either we pay now for effective law enforcement or we pay far more later to cope with the destruction caused by illegal drugs."

— District Attorney Robert M. Morgenthau

OPERATION STOP CROP

Of all the marijuana smoked in the United States, roughly 25 percent is produced by domestic growers. When asked to estimate the size of America's domestic marijuana crop, federal officials admit that nothing more than rough estimates are possible. But everyone agrees that production of homegrown marijuana is at an all-time high. U.S. marijuana production is believed to have tripled in recent years, from roughly 2.6 million pounds in 1981 to almost 8 million pounds in 1987, according to Drug Enforcement Administration (DEA) estimates. Some 100,000 commercial growers are engaged in the domestic marijuana-growing industry.

Throughout the early- and mid-1980s, marijuana cultivation was a misdemeanor, and government efforts to stop it consisted chiefly of periodic eradication efforts. With the passage of the 1986 drug act, marijuana cultivation was redefined as a felony charge. Since then, the government has stepped up efforts to stamp out homegrown cannabis.

In July 1988, the Justice Department announced what Attorney General Meese described as the nation's most intensive effort to destroy the marijuana crop. The campaign, called "Operation Stop Crop," consisted of expanded surveillance designed to locate crops, including aerial support from National Guard troops and helicopters. The campaign also provided a toll-free number to encourage citizen informers to identify growers.

Although several states — New Jersey, North Dakota, and Nevada — chose not to participate, local enforcement officials in 47 states joined federal agents in the effort, fanning out through suspected marijuana-growing areas, which officials said were often protected by elaborate booby traps, electric fences, and pit bulls. Prevented from using aerial sprays by recent lawsuits, agents destroyed marijuana crops manually, using machetes called brush axes.

Critics such as Arnold Trebach, professor of justice at the American University and president of the Drug Policy Foundation, a group critical of the nation's drug laws, ridiculed "Operation Stop Crop" as a waste of government resources. "These raids are going to be minimally effective," said Trebach. "There is no amount of military force that can be used in any civilized manner that can have a significant impact on the crop."

cent of their caseload. Fully one-third said that up to 50 percent of their caseload consists of prosecuting drug crimes.

From the perspective of this second choice, since current efforts to contain the domestic drug trade are clearly inadequate, more resources must be employed to root out this pernicious commerce. "So long as we are unable to suppress the sale of drugs," writes John Kaplan, "we will be remitting large parts of our cities to the terrorization of innocent people, drug-related killings, and the brutalization that comes from constant exposure to the use of drugs. Perhaps equally demoral-izing is the sight of a large number of teenage drug lords who own Jaguars or Ferraris before they are old enough to have drivers' licenses." By stepping up efforts to apprehend drug dealers, concludes Kaplan, "we can accomplish much more than we have."

FEEBLE RESPONSE

Proponents of this choice favor four measures to strengthen enforcement efforts. Law enforcement officials should be given more resources. Police should be given freer rein to search houses of people suspected of selling drugs. Penalties for drug sales should be made more stringent. And the death penalty should apply to any individual who kills in connection with drug-related activity.

With regard to the first of those measures, proponents of this choice are convinced that it is unrealistic to expect law enforcement officials to do more unless they are given more resources. Across the country, enforcement officials voice a gritty determination to fight the war on drugs. But with their current resources they are simply overwhelmed.

In the words of Robert M. Morgenthau, district attorney for the County of New York: "Those of us in state and local enforcement desperately need more resources. To date, my office has been promised only $700,000 — 20 percent of what is needed — to prosecute the truly massive increase in cases from the police department's new Tactical Narcotics Teams. Nor have adequate resources been budgeted for the courts or the correctional system. Underfunded programs will mean 'revolving door justice' in which dealers are arrested only to be returned to the streets."

"Never in my 20 years in public life," continues Morgenthau, "have I witnessed anything quite as disheartening as our feeble response to the illegal drug epidemic. At every level of government, rhetoric outstrips resources and commitment."

Morgenthau is critical of recent anti-drug initiatives on the grounds that they do not provide law enforcement officials with the resources they need. "The recently enacted Anti-Drug Abuse Law of 1988," he writes, "allocates precious little money for the essential task of punishing dealers. It is unlikely that the Drug Enforcement Administration or the FBI will add a single new agent to their drug enforcement squads. The choice is clear: either we pay now for effective law enforcement or we pay far more later to cope with the destruction caused by illegal drugs."

If law enforcement officials are to succeed in rooting out drug dealers, proponents of this strategy are convinced that they also need freer rein to search the houses of people suspected of selling drugs, without a court order. Moreover, police should be allowed to conduct random searches of cars. Advocates of such measures concede that allowing such searches means that the houses of innocent people may be searched by mistake and that cars of individuals who are not carrying drugs may be stopped and searched. But that is a small price to pay, they say, for a more effective war on drugs.

THE ULTIMATE PENALTY

A third measure favored by advocates of this approach is the imposition of swift and certain punishment — and longer sentences — on drug dealers. Currently, because of scarce resources, many drug dealers are placed on unsupervised probation, which amounts to little more than a slap on the wrist. Proponents of this approach insist that drug traffickers must know that, when convicted, they will pay the full penalty imposed by law for their offense. No one convicted of peddling drugs, even first offenders, should go unpunished.

In New York State, legislators recently approved more stringent penalties for crack dealers. Previously, dealers were able to escape long prison terms by carrying no more than a few vials of a highly concentrated drug. People who carried up to 30 vials of crack faced misdemeanor charges and a maximum jail sentence of just one year. The 1988 law makes possession of as few as six vials a felony that carries a penalty of up to seven years in prison. Governor Mario Cuomo said that the "alarming increase in the use of crack through the state, particularly in New York City, warrants the tougher penalties contained in the legislation."

In deliberations over the new drug bill, the 100th Congress was also concerned about imposing harsher penalties for convicted drug dealers. One of the measures favored by advocates of this approach — imposing the death penalty for drug dealers who commit murder — generated heated debate. Previously, the only crimes for which the death penalty could be imposed were espionage by military personnel and killings associated with an airline hijacking. In the House and the Senate, there was support for applying the death penalty to drug dealers as well.

Gang members arrested on drug charges in Los Angeles

BOB RIHA, GAMMA/LIAISON

In the Senate, the death penalty measure was introduced by Alfonse D'Amato, who explained that it is mainly aimed at "drug kingpins" who order killings in which they do not personally participate. A similar proposal in the House went farther, proposing the death penalty for murders committed during drug-related crime, whether by drug kingpins or anyone else engaged in the narcotics trade. Saying that the public "demanded" execution in such cases, Representative George Gekas asserted that "the war on drugs cannot be won without this ultimate penalty."

To proponents of stepped-up law enforcement efforts to win the war on drugs, the "ultimate penalty" is a way to serve notice to anyone who contemplates using violent measures while selling drugs. It is time, in the words of Representative James Traficant, Jr., who supported the death penalty proposal, "to fight fire with fire."

WHAT CRITICS SAY

Critics regard the clamor for capital punishment — which they view as a morally reprehensible sanction that has no proven ability to reduce violent crime — as an emblem of the growing tendency to resort to punitive measures to deal with the drug problem, regardless of their effectiveness. Unfortunately, because so many individuals are drawn to the drug trade, not much can be expected of efforts to reduce the number of drug merchants. Even if most of the current dealers were jailed, others are ready to take their places.

Time after time, when police crack down on drug sellers and proclaim their efforts a success, such efforts turn out to be less fruitful than anticipated. In December 1988, after police and drug authorities raided buildings in upper Manhattan that served as a

headquarters for drug dealers, it turned out that only eight people were arrested as a result of the operation, none of whom were major dealers. Mayor Koch's vaunted anti-crack strike force, known as the Tactical Narcotics Teams, has been criticized by a watch dog group, the Citizens Crime Commission, as a "unidimensional" effort that only drives dealers from one neighborhood to another, meanwhile clogging the courts with low-level dealers.

The experience of another New York City neighborhood supports that observation. In South Jamaica, Queens, residents report that crack dealers returned just two weeks after a 118-member tactical unit was moved from that neighborhood to a different part of the borough.

Even members of New York's police force admit that it is futile to try to solve the drug problem by stepping up enforcement efforts. "The thing that amazes me about narcotics," says Francis C. Hall, commander of the

police department's narcotics division, "is that it's the only crime about which people say, 'Why don't we eliminate it?' That's unrealistic. You know what I compare it to? The department of sanitation picks up our garbage every day, but they know there's going to be more garbage tomorrow. It's the same thing with narcotics."

Other cities have had similar experiences. Police in Washington, D.C., have conducted an aggressive effort to stamp out drugs. As a result of Operation Clean Sweep, Washington has the highest rate of drug-related arrests of any American city. Felons convicted of drug sales in D.C. spend more time behind bars than those in most cities — an average of 39 months, as opposed to a national rate of 16 months. Consequently, the city's prison population has increased by more than 50 percent over the past 5 years.

JIM MORIN, THE MIAMI HERALD

ED GAMBLE, *THE FLORIDA TIMES - UNION*

"HOLD YOUR FIRE...THIS IS WILLIAM J. BENNETT...THE NEW DRUG CZAR! YOU CAN FORGET THE 'JUST SAY NO' CAMPAIGN...WE REALLY MEAN BUSINESS THIS TIME.!!"

Despite the crackdown, Washington's drug problem grows worse. Since 1986, reported incidents of drug abuse have increased dramatically. Washington's drug abuse "hotline" is the busiest in the country. The crime rate is up too, driven by the drug trade. Homicides — many of which are drug-related — have more than doubled over the past few years. The most visible effect of the crackdown is that every aspect of Washington's judicial and corrections system is now strained to the breaking point.

In the words of a recent report conducted by the Rand Corporation, "The Washington-area heroin, PCP, and cocaine problem is worse than that of most comparable metropolitan areas. There is, unfortunately, little to suggest that enforcement has had many of the intended consequences."

STOPGAP OR SOLUTION

As a nation, we could take a more punitive approach to the drug problem and beef up enforcement efforts to fight a concerted war on drugs. But critics of this second choice conclude that there is little reason to think it will work.

Nonetheless, authorities in various parts of the country are escalating the war on drugs. Like their counterparts in Los Angeles and Chicago, some D.C. police now carry semiautomatic pistols with which they engage in bloody shoot-outs with drug dealers. Frustrated with the lack of results from Washington's aggressive anti-drug campaign, the District Council recently called on the National Guard to help in its efforts to defeat drug dealers.

Critics conclude that the war on drugs is escalating mindlessly, threatening the values we espouse as a society. In the words of David Boaz, vice-president of the Cato Institute, a public policy research organization, "It's time to ask ourselves: What kind of society would condone strip searches, large-scale arrests, military occupation of its capital city and the shooting of possibly innocent people in order to stop people from using substances that others don't like?"

In the debate over more stringent enforcement measures, some of the most notable criticism comes from the field generals of the legal system, the prosecutors who carry out drug policy. In a 1988 *National Law Journal* survey, when prosecutors were asked about the war on drugs, a majority agreed that current efforts are not succeeding in reducing the supply of drugs. Prosecutors were virtually unanimous in their conclusion that "clean sweeps" do nothing but drive dealers from one neighborhood to another. Despite extraordinary efforts that in many cases have overwhelmed the criminal justice system, two-thirds of the prosecutors said that enforcement efforts have little impact on narcotics.

According to the study, most prosecutors conclude that too much hope is placed on law enforcement as the answer to the drug problem. "There is no law enforcement answer to the drug problem," says New Hampshire's Rockingham County Attorney, Carlton Eldridge, articulating a widely shared view among prosecutors. "This is just a stopgap. We're not getting down to root causes."

A different approach to the problem is to reduce the demand for drugs, which is the strategy to which we now turn. ■

CHOICE #3
SAYING NO: TARGETING USERS, REDUCING DEMAND

"Currently, some 23 million Americans regularly use drugs. The war on drugs can be won only by persuading them to stop, and by persuading potential drug users not to start."

Throughout the summer and fall of 1988, as members of Congress considered the provisions of the new anti-drug law, there was increasing support for the position that neither stepped-up interdiction efforts nor tougher criminal sanctions would solve the drug problem. As long as people are eager to buy drugs, said former Senator Paula Hawkins, narcotics agents will be "outspent, outgunned, and outmanned by the drug underground."

During the Reagan administration, the First Lady was the most influential spokesperson for efforts to curb demand. "It is often easier," said Mrs. Reagan in an October 1988 address at the United Nations, "to make strong speeches about foreign drug lords or drug smugglers than to arrest a pair of Wall Street investment bankers buying cocaine on their lunch break."

In that speech, Nancy Reagan reiterated the importance of teaching young people to "Just Say No" to drugs. But she also advocated tough measures to curb demand. "If we lack the will to fully mobilize the forces of law to arrest and punish drug users, if we cannot stem the American demand for drugs, then there will be little hope of preventing foreign drug producers from filling that demand."

Advocates of this approach are convinced, as Mrs. Reagan repeatedly asserted, that casual users who create a climate of acceptance for drugs are accomplices in the problem. Moreover, allowing users to escape punishment conveys the message that society is not very serious about discouraging drugs, thus encouraging others to experiment. For these reasons, society must be intolerant of drug use anywhere, anytime, by anybody.

From this perspective, the war on drugs can be won only by persuading users to turn off, and by persuading potential drug users not to turn on in the first place. If a substantial fraction of the 23 million Americans who currently use illicit drugs at least once a month can be persuaded to stop, the drug market will shrink, sparing potential victims of drug-related crime.

Accordingly, advocates of this approach favor various measures intended to reduce the demand for drugs, ranging from expanded drug education and treatment to mandatory drug testing, and punitive measures targeted at users including arrest, fines, seizure of property, forfeiture of drivers' licenses and other privileges.

The key phrases in this approach are "zero tolerance" and "user accountability," which means that even casual users of drugs need to know that their behavior is unacceptable, and that they will be held accountable for using illegal substances.

DRUG-FREE SCHOOLS

In the effort to reduce demand for drugs, the first requirement is a well-orchestrated effort to change public attitudes, especially the inclination of young people to experiment with drugs. "As soon as we can and as early as we can" said New York Governor Mario Cuomo early in 1989, "we must teach our children not to take drugs, not even to try them. In our schools, in our churches, in our synagogues, on television, on billboards, every way that we can, everywhere that we can, we must teach children not to take drugs."

Proponents of this strategy point to progress in discouraging use of two drugs that are legal — alcohol and tobacco. As a result of educational campaigns emphasizing health hazards, the number of cigarette

ABUSED SUBSTANCES:
FACTS ABOUT DRUG AND ALCOHOL USE

American society is awash in substances used by millions of Americans to produce alterations in body or mind — including illicit drugs, prescription drugs, and such commonly used substances as cigarettes and alcohol. This is a profile of drug and alcohol use.

THE MOST ABUSED SUBSTANCE

As prevalent as illicit drugs have become, alcohol, which is used regularly by 113 million Americans is the most widely abused substance. There are more alcoholics than drug addicts. The National Clearinghouse on Alcohol Information estimates that 10 million Americans — including some 4 million adolescents — are problem drinkers. Alcohol-related diseases and accidents kill far more people than drugs do.

Last year, more than half of all traffic fatalities were alcohol-related. Alcoholism is the principal cause of accidental death among those in the age category 15 through 24. Furthermore, the Department of Health and Human Services reports that alcohol is a factor in about half of all cases of marital violence.

ALCOHOL ABUSE

Alcohol is the drug of preference on college campuses, and beer is the most popular alcoholic beverage. Beer contains about 4-6 percent alcohol. So a 12-ounce can of beer contains one-half ounce of alcohol — about the same amount as a glass of wine or liquor.

According to a recent National Institute of Drug Abuse (NIDA) Adolescent Health Survey, 89 percent of tenth grad-

ers say that they have consumed alcoholic beverages at some point, and 53 percent report that they have had an alcoholic beverage during the past month. Thirty-eight percent of tenth graders report having had five or more drinks on at least one occasion over the past two weeks.

ROY MORSCH/THE STOCK MARKET

AT LEAST ONCE

Taking illicit drugs is by no means the habit of a small, deviant minority. According to the National Institute on Drug Abuse, some 62 million Americans have tried marijuana at least once in their lifetimes, and 22 million Americans have tried cocaine.

REGULAR USERS

Some 23 million Americans use illicit drugs at least once a month. There are 18 million regular users of marijuana, 6 million regular users of cocaine, 3 million regular users of stimulants, 2 mil-

lion regular users of inhalants, and 1 million regular users of hallucinogens.

DRUG USE

In 1988, NIDA released results from a study of 11,000 high school students. Studies that ask respondents to report on illicit activities undoubtedly underestimate those activities. Still, the NIDA report provides the most accurate profile to date of substance abuse among American adolescents. It shows that while drug use among high school students has declined somewhat over the past few years, more than half of American youth (58 percent) try an illicit drug before they finish high school.

MARIJUANA AND COCAINE

Marijuana use among young people has declined somewhat over the past ten years. However, nearly six in ten high school students said it is easy for them to buy marijuana, and 50 percent of high school students use marijuana at least once before they graduate. Among 13-year-olds, 1 in 6 reports using marijuana, the highest figure ever recorded for this age group. While overall use of marijuana is declining, its use among young teenagers is more common today.

Twenty-seven percent of America's high school students report that it is relatively easy to buy cocaine if they choose to do so. Fifteen percent of students use cocaine at least once before they graduate. Of those who have tried cocaine, approximately one-third have tried crack. Three percent of high school students report having used cocaine once or more during the past month.

> *"As soon as we can and as early as we can, we must teach our children not to take drugs, not even to try them."*
>
> — Governor Mario Cuomo

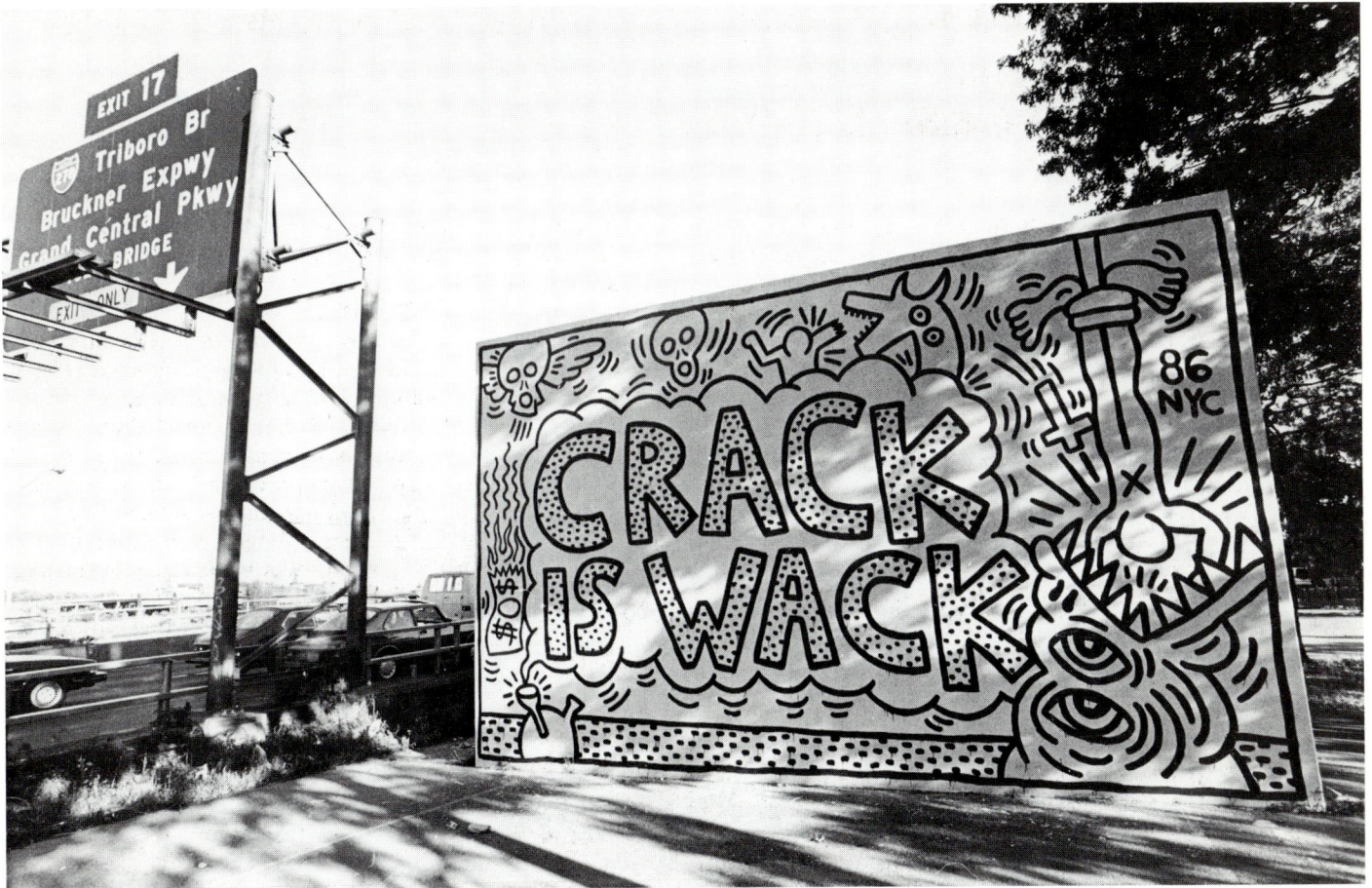

TANNENBAUM/SYGMA

smokers has gradually declined over the past decade. Similarly, anti-alcohol campaigns have convinced drinkers to reduce alcohol consumption, to switch from spirits to wine. There is reason to believe that a concerted campaign against drug use could be equally effective.

What goes on in the schools is particularly important in reducing demand. In the words of former Secretary of Education and current "drug czar" William Bennett, "In America today, the most serious threat to the health and well-being of our children is drug use. . . . Drug use is at alarming levels. Even more troubling is the fact that children are using drugs at younger ages."

The Department of Education issued a report in 1987 on what schools can do to help with the drug problem. The report, entitled *What Works: Schools Without Drugs*, recommended that schools develop a comprehensive drug prevention curriculum for kindergarten through grade 12, teaching that drug use is wrong and helping students to resist drugs. In many school systems, students at every level receive some form of education about drug abuse. In particular, advocates of this approach favor efforts to use peers to teach young children techniques for dealing with social pressures to buy and use drugs.

Efforts to involve the schools in the anti-drug effort are generally well received. Indeed, polls show that education is the most popular method

for dealing with drugs. But other initiatives proposed in the report from Secretary Bennett's office are more controversial. Insisting that school principals should clearly establish that drug possession will not be tolerated on school grounds or at school functions, the report advises school officials to "do everything they can to determine whether school grounds are being used to facilitate the possession, use, or distribution of drugs, and to prevent such crimes."

"Everything they can" includes drug searches, and that has become a controversial topic. The issue arose when officials in some schools conducted unannounced searches of such areas as student lockers, bathrooms, and "smoking areas" where they suspected drugs were used or stored. Some students and parents objected on the grounds that such actions violate a citizen's constitutional protection against unwarranted search and seizure. On several occasions, however, the courts have upheld the right of school officials to conduct searches that would not be permitted if conducted by police officers or in the larger community.

Proponents of this strategy are convinced that drug-free schools are essential as a first line of defense. School administrators should not condone the presence of drugs anywhere on school property. Unless they are allowed to conduct such searches, they cannot guarantee a drug-free environment.

ZERO TOLERANCE

Zero tolerance means more than drug-free schools. To advocates of measures to reduce demand, it also means getting serious about small-time users. Currently, although possession of small amounts of such substances as marijuana or cocaine is a punishable offense, most individuals who are arrested for drug possession pay no more than a small fine.

Proponents of this approach insist upon serious sanctions for all drug users. Donald I. Macdonald, White House drug adviser in the Reagan administration, advocated the arrest of small-time users — lawyers with a quarter gram of cocaine, high school students with a couple of joints — and bringing them before a judge.

That approach was illustrated by Project Zero Tolerance, which was implemented by the administration in 1988. The White House instructed the Coast Guard, the Customs Service, and other federal agencies to enforce laws on drug possession to the letter. The policy's objective, explained

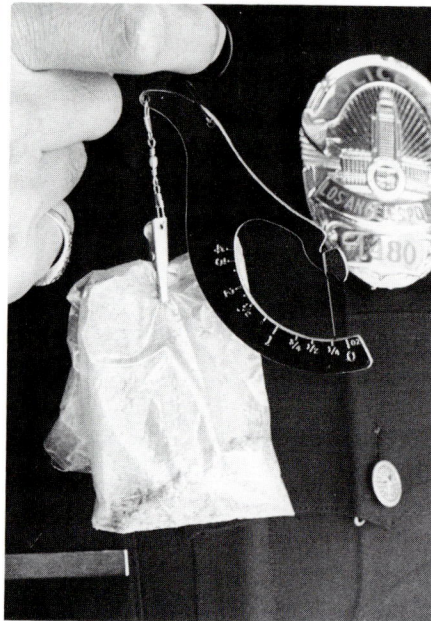

Police in Los Angeles carry pocket-sized scales to weigh drugs seized from small-time users.

Customs Commissioner William von Raab, is to put pressure on drug users who ordinarily are not affected by drug laws.

Authorities used a procedure called "administrative seizures" to seize vehicles on which just a trace of illegal substances is found. Within a matter of weeks, officials seized more than 1,000 cars, planes, and boats — including the $2.5 million yacht *Ark Royal*.

Later in 1988, members of the House and Senate had "zero tolerance" and "user accountability" in mind when they approved new sanctions for drug offenders, including the denial of federal benefits such as access to public housing and job training programs. Explaining those measures, Senator Phil Gramm said that "the real drug kingpin is the user. It is the casual users who create the profits."

But we can't put them all into jail." Referring to the civil penalties in the new bill, he said, "We have to use disincentives."

Similarly, advocates of this approach are convinced that judges should stop accepting drug addiction as an extenuating circumstance for individuals who commit other crimes. Whether they are heroin-using burglars or muggers under the influence of crack, drug-using offenders should be required to stop using drugs as a condition for receiving bail or parole. The only way to win the war on drugs, conclude advocates of this strategy, is to use every tool at our disposal to create incentives to avoid drugs.

TESTING SOLUTION

Proponents of reducing the demand for drugs feel that it is appropriate to insist upon testing — in the military, in the workplace, and in the schools. Since drug use is not easy to detect, testing is the only way to ensure that people remain drug free. It is also an effective deterrent to drug use.

Proponents of testing as a way to reduce demand point to what happened after the Armed Forces began conducting random urine tests several years ago. Prior to the use of those tests, 27 percent of military personnel surveyed admitted that they had used drugs during the previous 30 days. After the testing program began, only 9 percent gave the same answer. In the words of Julian Barber, a Pentagon health official, "The word has gone out to 2.2 million men and women in uniform. If you want to stay in, stop taking drugs."

The Reagan administration's 1986 "drug-free workplace" initiative mandated random drug testing for persons in sensitive positions throughout the federal bureaucracy, which by

WHAT SHOULD BE DONE ABOUT DRUG-ABUSING ATHLETES?

Excerpted with permission from an editorial by Representative Charles Rangel, Chairman of the House Select Committee on Narcotics Abuse and Control, (Washington Post, September 20, 1988).

The professional football season is now in full swing, and the most newsworthy events at the start unfortunately are occurring off the field rather than on it. The best player in the league — Lawrence Taylor, the pride of New York and the Giants — begins the season on the sidelines sacked by drugs. Again.

The case of this talented, stellar young man is a dreadful sign of the times in professional sports as athletes from various sports continue to trip up on illicit drugs, mirroring what is going on throughout society. Already, after the first couple weeks of play, no fewer than 18 other NFL players have joined Taylor on the dubious All-Drug Team. It has become sheer folly. These guys get caught using drugs, then the tough-talking commissioners, vowing to "clean up the sport," slap the players on the wrist not once, but twice.

Only after repeated missteps by the players do the commissioners do anything tough, such as levy lifetime bans. Even that is a misnomer, since the major sports allow players to petition for reinstatement after a year or two out.

The fact of the matter is that in America, if you run, block, and tackle well, can slam-dunk a basketball, have just the right grip on a tennis racket or can stroke line drives or throw a baseball

MERCURY MORRIS

AND THEN I GOT BUSTED.

There was this guy, a nationally known sports hero. And then I got busted. As a result of my lust for cocaine, I bypassed high and went straight to messed up. I mean zoom— there was no stopping. Some of you know exactly what I'm talking about because you're taking the exact same ride. A phone call could help you. It took prison to help me.

COCAINE. THE BIG LIE. 1-800-662-HELP.

THE ADVERTISING COUNCIL, INC.

well, your drug abuse is excused and accepted.

Such treatment is unfair on its face, since most ordinary people in society pay a heavy price socially, professionally, and personally when their drug use is discovered.

Most importantly, wrist-slappings administered to athletes offer little deterrence to others who may consider experimenting with illegal drugs, especially to the youngsters who worship these supposed role models. They must assume from the lightweight penalties accorded professional athletes that drug use is okay. We should not mislead society into thinking that drug use in sports is taken less seriously than in other walks of life.

When the main concern about an athlete's drug suspension is "Will he be back in time for the big game?" we have all committed a foul — against the player and against society by moving ourselves farther away from the goal of a drug-free America. It's easy to see why such selfish feelings abound. Many of these guys are top-quality performers. But is it really fair to them to keep giving them strolls down Easy Street until they reach the dead end? It seems that in every case, a player should get the entire season off — whether you call it a suspension or a vacation. At least that much time is needed to soundly recover, and having to sit out at least a year without pay is enough to make anyone think twice before using drugs.

When athletes get preferential treatment, little is accomplished. The light penalties given drug-using sports stars look and sound good to the general public, but in the end, they really don't help in fighting the "war on drugs" or in aiding the individuals involved.

"CONGRATULATIONS, HENDERSON!...YOU CAME OUT QUITE HIGH ON THE EMPLOYEE TEST— UNFORTUNATELY IT WAS THE DRUG TEST!"

MARLETTE, *THE CHARLOTTE OBSERVER*

one estimate included half of the government's 2.2 million civilian employees. In 1988, the initiative was expanded to require mandatory drug testing of about 4 million workers in the airline, railroad, trucking, mass transit, and maritime industries. President Reagan urged private business leaders to follow the lead of the federal government in using random testing to ensure a drug-free workplace.

Currently, private sector employers are more eager to weed out drug users before they join the company than to test for drug use among current employees. According to a recent Labor Department study, only 1 percent of American workers were tested for drug use in 1988. Of the roughly 1 million tests reported, 9 percent showed evidence of drug use. In the industries where drug testing is most common — mining, public utilities, and transportation — the percentage of employees testing positive was well below that figure, presumably because users in those industries became more cautious.

To proponents of more aggressive

measures to stop drug use, the Labor Department study suggests that testing is useful, both as a way of identifying employees with drug problems and as a way to serve notice that drug use will not be tolerated. Since drug use affects productivity, leads to on-the-job accidents, and contributes to absenteeism, employers have a right to insist that workers remain drug free.

In some companies, a "zero tolerance" policy is taken literally, and workers who test positive for drugs are dismissed. The Georgia Power Company in Atlanta, for example, tests employees whenever supervisors suspect drug use. "Once employees are asked to take a drug test," says the company's health services manager, "it's too late. There's zero tolerance when someone tests positive."

DRUG TREATMENT

Proponents of curbing the drug problem by reducing demand also strongly favor providing drug treatment to anyone who needs it. As they see it, a sensible program would

offer a range of approaches — including residential centers and therapeutic communities, outpatient therapy, and substitute drugs like methadone.

Advocates of expanded drug treatment programs acknowledge that this is an expensive alternative. Yearly costs range from several thousand dollars per person for drug-free outpatient programs to fifteen thousand dollars a year or more for addicts in long-term residential programs. However, proponents of curbing the drug problem by reducing demand believe providing drug treatment facilities is an investment worth making. A three-year study by the National Institute on Drug Abuse found that methadone treatment programs are successful in reducing intravenous drug use. Most importantly, drug treatment programs focus on the heaviest users, who are most responsible for keeping sellers in business and who commit the most crimes to support their habits. When treatment programs are properly run, they are an effective way to curtail heavy users' demand for drugs.

Yet despite heightened funding for treatment provided by the Anti-Drug Abuse Acts of 1986 and 1988, treatment programs have been chronically underfunded. Though federal funds for treatment have increased as a share of the federal drug budget, spending for this purpose declined from 19 percent in 1981 to 14 percent in 1988. Only 150,000 of an estimated 1.4 million intravenous drug users currently receive treatment.

Because of intensive enforcement and widespread use of crack, a highly addictive substance, demand for drug treatment has substantially increased. Currently, there is a long waiting list for treatment in many cities. In New York City, for example, there are three times as many addicts who want treatment as there are spaces, and the wait for treatment can be as long as six months.

Advocates of expanded drug treatment point out that this is a serious problem, since addicts need immediate treatment. "An addict is used to taking heroin and getting immediate relief," says David Turner, director of London's Conference on Drug Abuse. "It is not surprising that if he is told he can have an appointment in four weeks, he will probably forget about it."

Proponents of this strategy conclude that it is necessary not only to mount a serious effort to reduce the demand for drugs but also to increase funding for drug treatment. Something else is necessary, the political will to put treatment clinics in neighborhoods despite the opposition of local residents to such facilities.

Advocates of significantly expanded drug treatment facilities acknowledge that this is a slow and expensive way to decrease the demand for drugs. Still, they say it is a more promising way to beat the drug problem than calling out the military to thwart drug suppliers or putting more public resources into law enforcement.

WHAT CRITICS SAY

The goal of reducing drug use commands virtually universal support. But some people are less than enthusiastic about the measures proposed by advocates of a "zero tolerance" policy. Critics of this approach are doubtful that such humane approaches as treatment, rehabilitation, and education make much of a difference.

Since drug education requires no coercion and is relatively inexpensive, it is an attractive alternative. But a recent study from the government's General Accounting Office (GAO) suggests that the results of anti-drug education programs are modest at best. Most educational strategies have three objectives: they are designed to increase students' knowledge about drugs; to heighten awareness of the adverse consequences; and to lessen the need for drugs by increasing self-esteem.

After examining the effects of such programs, the GAO concluded that while some programs are successful in increasing knowledge, "few had demonstrated any degree of success in preventing drug abuse." While practitioners of anti-drug education efforts are enthusiastic, the worth of this approach remains to be proved.

Similarly, while few people are critical of efforts to expand drug treatment, many are skeptical about the prospects of a treatment-centered approach. Substitute drugs such as methadone help heroin addicts. But methadone is ineffective in treating cocaine or crack addiction. Such patients have to rely upon programs that use individual or group therapy — a process that is both costly and lengthy — rather than substitute drugs. Drug treatment experts in many cities report that the majority of crack addicts who enter treatment facilities leave before the program is complete.

Consequently, current treatment methods offer faint hope to cocaine and crack addicts. In the words of drug expert Peter Reuter, "The fact is, treatment techniques for cocaine are not very good. It's fair to say that if you spend large sums of money on cocaine treatment right now, you won't have much to show for it in terms of reduction of cocaine users. You might have something to show for it in five years — it's that kind of time frame."

MIKE LANE, *THE EVENING SUN*

TESTING CONTROVERSY: DRUG TESTING AT HOME AND IN THE SCHOOLS

As concern over adolescent drug use grows, debate intensifies about whether young people should be tested to determine if they are drug free. In San Angelo, Texas, a voluntary testing program has been in effect for several years in the high schools. Students are asked to return consent forms indicating that they agree to be tested for the presence of drugs in urine samples. When tests are positive, parents are asked to participate in joint student-parent counseling sessions. After several positive tests, students are referred to treatment and rehabilitation programs.

Though some parents initially opposed San Angelo's voluntary testing program, it is now widely supported by students, parents, and school administrators. Students generally accept the testing program and are happy to prove that they are drug free.

Some drug-abuse experts favor the use of school testing programs such as San Angelo's. "Since the signs of drug use are not always clear in young people," says psychiatrist and former White House drug adviser Robert DuPont, "testing is the only way for parents and teachers to know for sure. Testing helps to identify the students with drug problems, and it has tremendous deterrent value. If a kid knows he's going to be tested, he's much less likely to use drugs." Considering what is at stake, says DuPont, "testing involves a small loss of privacy and a large gain both for the individual and for the community."

"The key to dealing with the drug epidemic," says DuPont, "is helping kids understand that drug use will not be tolerated. Testing is one of the best ways to convey that message. I think testing programs like the one in San Angelo are a wonderful first step. The next step is

mandatory testing of all kids as a precondition for participation in school, like testing for tuberculosis and other contagious diseases."

Many people object to drug testing in the schools on the grounds that it violates Fourth Amendment rights. "When a kid is disruptive or deals drugs on school premises, that's one thing," says

1 out of 2 teens in America has taken drugs. 1 out of 2 parents doesn't see it.

See, the Washingtons think it's the Smith kid. The Smiths think it's the Sanchez kid. Maybe the Sanchezes think it's your kid. Maybe it is your kid. Find out. Talk to your kids. Tell 'em the dangers of drugs. Tell 'em how to handle peer pressure.

Tell 'em you care. It's not easy. But I can help. So write me, McGruff, P.O. Box 562, Washington, D.C. 20004. Don't let your kids take a powder. Or anything else. Together, we can help Take a Bite out of Crime.

TAKE A BITE OUT OF CRIME

THE ADVERTISING COUNCIL, INC.

ACLU attorney Loren Siegel. "In that case, the school has a right and a responsibility to test kids to find out whether they are doing drugs. But it's a very bad idea for kids to be told they have to waive their right to privacy to participate in extracurricular activity or school itself. At that point, Fourth Amendment protections begin to unravel. Moreover, the tests aren't 100 percent accurate. If you subject millions of kids to mandatory drug tests, the false positives will out-

number the instances in which actual drug use is detected, with incredibly destructive results."

In Atlanta, there is a new development in the controversy over testing adolescents for drug use. A program initiated by psychiatrist Dirk Huttenbach encourages parents who believe their children are using drugs to take urine samples at home and have them tested at participating hospitals. Huttenbach says that the value of home testing is that it allows parents to determine whether their children are using drugs. Parents can use the threat of further tests to convince them to stop. In Huttenbach's words, "If every child and parent knows this test is easily available, it's bound to have a deterrent effect."

Robert DuPont agrees about the value of parent-administered drug tests. "Parents should make it clear that they have a right to test their kids. Parents who assume that they can trust their children just because they are nice kids aren't being realistic. I think home testing is a positive thing. Drugs destroy kids and tear down the relationship between parents and kids. Kids are basically looking to adults to act like adults. Testing lets them do this."

Like widespread drug testing in schools, home testing is criticized by health authorities and civil libertarians who are convinced that it deprives children of their dignity while invading their privacy. "We regard this as an ominous sign of drug war hysteria," says Loren Siegel. "Home testing creates suspicion in families. It's a very destructive and anti-family way to approach the problem of drugs. As for the effectiveness of testing as a deterrent, that is still unclear."

> **"If we really try to become a drug-free society and use every means to do so, we may end up being a 'rights-free' society."**
> — Arnold Trebach

EFFECTS OF PUNITIVE MEASURES

Critics have a different response to the punitive measures proposed by advocates of reducing the demand for drugs. They are concerned about mandatory or widespread drug testing for two reasons.

Some people are chiefly concerned about the unreliability of drug tests and the possibility that mistaken test results could ruin a worker's reputation or chances for advancement. Others are concerned that random testing amounts to a serious invasion of privacy. For each inch gained in the war on drugs by taking such measures, they are convinced that we lose a substantial fraction of our civil liberties. "If we really try to become a drug-free society and use every means to do so," says Arnold Trebach, "we may end up being a 'rights-free' society."

Moreover, massive drug testing could have the paradoxical effect of prodding individuals to shift from marijuana, which stays in the urine for a week or longer, to cocaine or crack, which leaves traces in urine for only two or three days — or to alcohol, which is not detected by drug tests.

Critics of "zero tolerance" point out that it amounts to throwing resources indiscriminately at drug users. "The problem with the present anti-drug culture," writes *Washington Post* columnist Richard Cohen, "is that it's the mirror opposite of the permissive drug culture that preceded it. Where once all drugs were touted as wonderful and harmless, now all drugs are equally condemned. . . . Administration officials are trying to send a message: drugs are bad and they will not be tolerated. Bully for them. Who can argue? But because the message is as indiscriminate as the programs being implemented, its consequences may ultimately be counterproductive."

JIM MORIN, *THE MIAMI HERALD*

Over the past few years, arrests for the possession of marijuana have accounted for the bulk of all drug arrests in this country. The question is whether it is counterproductive to spend such a large fraction of the nation's enforcement efforts going after individuals who use marijuana, while stinting on efforts to deal with more addictive and destructive substances.

"It is not sensible," said attorney Marvin Miller, in congressional testimony, "to devote so much of our enforcement budget to suppression of a relatively benign substance such as marijuana while letting those addicted to severely debilitating drugs such as crack and cocaine go untreated for lack of resources."

Drug policy in Texas provides an example of the perverse effects of zealous enforcement. Texas is one of the few states where individuals have been prosecuted for the possession of even small amounts of marijuana. Miller points out that Texas has spent as much as $50 million annually to punish individuals who possess marijuana. "The cost of the prohibition policy and punishment was considerable. Not only were taxpayer dollars expended to little effect, but a lot of damage was done to the private lives of otherwise law-abiding citizens." Despite those punishments, Miller concluded, such aggressive prosecution had "little noticeable effect" in reducing marijuana use in Texas.

We could pursue all drug users aggressively, justifying efforts such as the seizure of personal property whenever illicit substances are detected in the name of "zero tolerance." But many people feel that such measures are excessive. "We have a rule in American jurisprudence," says Colleen O'Connor of the American Civil Liberties Union, "that the penalty fits the crime. Confiscation of millions of dollars of property for a joint doesn't fit." Critics of measures designed to reduce the demand for drugs are concerned that public pressure for fast results will translate into efforts that are ineffective, and needlessly intrusive.

Some people are convinced that rather than trying to prevent all drug use by all people at all costs, it makes more sense to take drug distribution away from criminals — to regulate drug sales and treat drug abuse as a public health problem. That is the point of departure for our fourth choice. ■

CHOICE #4
LEGALIZING DRUGS: WHY PROHIBITION DOESN'T WORK

"The drug laws cause more damage than illicit substances themselves. A more sensible alternative is a policy that legalizes drugs, controls their distribution, and discourages their use."

A new phase in the drug debate began in April 1988, when Baltimore Mayor Kurt Schmoke addressed the U.S. Conference on Mayors and made the case for what had been a virtually unspeakable alternative — legalizing drugs. In his previous position as prosecutor, Schmoke won thousands of convictions for drug-related crimes, an experience that convinced him that better law enforcement is no solution to the drug problem. "Going to jail," he said, "is just part of the cost of doing business. It's a nuisance, not a deterrent."

Exasperated by the seemingly endless crime and corruption generated by the illegal drug trade, Schmoke concluded that efforts to beat the problem by making drugs illegal are doomed. From his perspective, what has happened since the Harrison Narcotics Act went into effect in 1914 shows that laws against drugs are ineffective and counterproductive. Drug laws lead to more severe problems than those directly associated with drug use.

"Have we failed to consider the lessons of the Prohibition era?" asked Schmoke. "Now is the time to fight on the only terms the drug underground empire respects — money. Let's take the profit out of drug trafficking." Concluding his speech to the Conference of Mayors, Schmoke called for a national debate on legalization.

Critics, who accused Schmoke of capitulating to drug dealers, said that legalization amounts to condoning drug use. Schmoke and others who favor this strategy reply that they do not condone drugs and they certainly don't want to encourage their use. But they are persuaded of the need to radically rethink the drug problem, and they are convinced that a strategy which legalizes drugs is far more likely to succeed than existing anti-drug efforts.

From this perspective, the current situation bears a striking resemblance to what happened in the 1920s, when a law prohibiting the manufacture and consumption of alcohol was in effect. The effort was doomed long before Prohibition was repealed in 1933. Similarly, advocates of legalization are convinced that drug prohibition should end. A more sensible alternative is a policy which legalizes drugs, controls their distribution, and discourages their use.

"Legalization of the drug market, like legalization of the alcohol market in the 1930s," says Ethan Nadelmann, a prominent advocate of this view, "would drive the drug-dealing business off the streets and out of the apartment buildings and into legal, government-regulated, taxpaying stores."

Proponents of this choice advocate a variety of proposals. Some people would stop short of full legalization and opt for eliminating criminal penalties for the use of drugs. Others would allow the sale of narcotics in much the same way that alcohol is sold. Dealers would be licensed, sales would be taxed and regulated, and dealers would be forbidden to sell to anyone under 21 years old.

Similarly, there are differences about which drugs should be made legally available. Some people favor legalizing marijuana but not other drugs. Economist Milton Friedman would allow the sale of "uppers" and "downers" at neighborhood drug stores. Attorney Alan Dershowitz proposes the free distribution of heroin from mobile vans in inner cities to "medically certified addicts." For his part, Schmoke told a congressional panel that he favors decriminalizing marijuana in tandem with a program of doctor-prescribed cocaine and heroin maintenance for addicts.

For all the differences among such proposals, the essence of this strategy is to make at least some currently illegal substances available to adults, to regulate their production and sale, to provide drug treatment to anyone who needs it, and to educate young people about drugs to discourage use.

PERVERSE EFFECTS

The argument for legalization begins with the assertion that current drug laws cause far more damage to society than illicit substances themselves. Laws intended to prohibit the trafficking, sale, and use of drugs are ineffective in keeping anyone who wants cocaine, heroin, marijuana, or a dozen other drugs from getting them. But the laws have perverse effects that are seriously at odds with their intention.

Most importantly, the laws significantly increase the price of drugs. The cost of producing most illicit drugs is no higher than the cost of producing coffee, tobacco, or alcohol. Most of the price paid for these substances amounts to an exorbitant tax levied by underground dealers. Consequently, the chief beneficiaries of the drug laws are the criminal organizations that profit from the drug trade.

Like bootleggers who made overnight fortunes during Prohibition, criminals benefit from sky-high drug prices. According to a report prepared for the President's Commission on Organized Crime, the sale of illicit drugs was the source of more than half of all organized crime revenues in 1986. Annually, marijuana and heroin sales each generate over $7 billion, and the cocaine business generates more than $13 billion.

One argument for legalization is that it would take away a substantial part of the profit that now fuels criminal organizations and entices individuals into the drug trade. "If we do not legalize products for which there is a huge demand," says policy analyst Lester Thurow, "profits will remain enormous. Since our goal is to deprive criminals of large profits from selling drugs, economic theory and history teach us that legalization is the only answer. When liquor sales were legalized after Prohibition, criminals left the bootleg industry because the huge profits available when the government was attempting to stop liquor sales vanished."

Beyond the black market prices that result from enforcing the prohibitions on drugs, the laws have other perverse effects. They generate crime and violence, as dealers fight over turf and sales, and drug users steal to buy illicit substances at inflated prices. Moreover, they encourage disrespect for the law by branding behavior practiced by more than 20 million Americans as criminal activity.

A final problem caused by prohibition is the health risk to drug users who have no assurance of what they get when they purchase drugs on the street. When you buy legal drugs in a pharmacy, you know something about the purity of the substance as well as the proper dosage, and you can assume that the label is accurate.

When you buy on the street, however, all bets are off. What you purchase may be different from what you

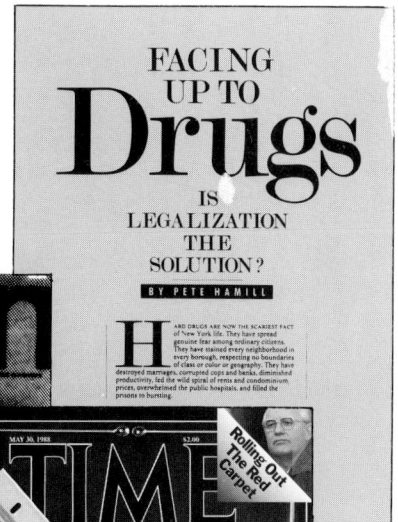

FACING UP TO Drugs IS LEGALIZATION THE SOLUTION?

BY PETE HAMILL

THE REASON FOUNDATION

NEW YORK

TIME INC.

33

are promised. The capsules may contain nothing more than a harmless filler. Or, as many drug users discover, the contents may be quite harmful. Nowhere is the phrase *caveat emptor* — let the buyer beware — more appropriate than for individuals who purchase illegal drugs.

Because the underground drug market is unregulated, there is no quality control. Consequently, people suffer from overdoses because the drugs they bought were impure or stronger than they suspected. In other cases, marijuana sprayed with paraquat or other pesticides is sold to unwary customers who suffer serious health consequences.

During Prohibition, police were unable to halt the production of alcohol.

UPI/BETTMAN NEWSPHOTOS

THE CRACK EPIDEMIC

In the words of Nobel prize winner, Milton Friedman: "The harm done by drugs is predominantly caused by the fact that they are illegal. We wouldn't have had the crack epidemic if drugs were legal."

How did the illegality of drugs lead to the crack epidemic? Studies from the National Institute of Drug Abuse show that the first drug many people buy is marijuana. But the underground drug market is interested in selling whatever is easiest to smuggle into the country, whatever produces the highest profit.

Marijuana leaves much to be desired from the seller's perspective. Because it is bulky, it is relatively easy to detect in transit. The street price of marijuana is not as high as other drugs. In contrast, crack is an ideal substance from the seller's perspective. It is relatively cheap to produce, easy to move, and it is very profitable. Unlike marijuana, it creates an addicted customer. Judging by the nationwide crack epidemic, the underground market has been successful in persuading marijuana buyers to switch to crack.

As proponents of legalization see it, the crack epidemic provides a vivid illustration of laws that lead to the opposite of their intended effect. Rather than deterring drug use or making sure that users stick to less dangerous substances, the laws encourage an underground market that aggressively promotes the sale and use of highly addictive substances.

In contrast, drug policy in the Netherlands shows how legalization of some substances keeps users of marijuana and hashish from moving on to harder drugs. In the early 1970s, in an effort to deal with a growing drug addiction problem, the Dutch government imposed more severe jail terms for trafficking in hard drugs. At the

> "Now is the time to fight on the only terms the drug underground empire respects — money. Let's take the profit out of drug trafficking."
> — Baltimore Mayor Kurt Schmoke

same time, officials announced that they would not prosecute anyone carrying less than 30 grams of marijuana or hashish.

Ever since, small amounts of hashish and marijuana have been sold more or less openly by coffeehouse operators in Amsterdam, under the watchful eye of the police. In the words of one Dutch drug policy adviser, "We're interested in keeping a small market of soft drugs so people will know where to get them." Law enforcement officials step in only when coffeehouse proprietors offer hard drugs. The result of this experiment is that curious young people can buy pot in small amounts and use it in a safe place, without being exposed to criminals who push hard drugs.

Some people feared that this experiment, which began more than a decade ago, would lead to a surge in marijuana use. But no such thing happened. Dutch officials believe that talking and acting openly about drugs has reduced their mystique and their attraction. The big payoff is that heroin use, the preferred hard drug in the Netherlands, has declined, especially among young people.

Dutch officials still go after traffickers and dealers in hard drugs, and users who commit crimes to support a habit are prosecuted. But rather than arresting cocaine and heroin users, Dutch authorities provide treatment for them. Like alcoholics, they are regarded as people who have medical problems.

So far, the experiment seems to be working. Proponents of legalizing drugs regard the Dutch model as a striking example of the promise of controlling the use of the most addictive drugs by tolerating and regulating less dangerous substances. The Dutch experiment is a pointed reminder that repealing drug laws does not necessarily lead to a dramatic rise in drug abuse.

New York City Police Commissioner Benjamin Ward with cash and weapons confiscated from a Colombian drug ring that did a $1 million per day business in the New York metropolitan area.

BENEFITS OF LEGALIZATION

Advocates of this choice are convinced that legalizing drugs would lead to benefits of several kinds. If drugs were legal, government could regulate their sale and set a low price. Consequently, the criminal industry that has profited from the drug trade would lose a major source of revenue. The pervasive corruption of police officers and judges bribed with drug money would come to an end. Drug gangs would gradually disappear, just as bootleggers vanished when Prohibition was repealed.

As the profits of the illegal drug trade dwindled, drug dealing would no longer represent the quickest way out of the ghetto for underclass youths. In the words of Mayor Schmoke, "If you take the profit out of drug trafficking, you wouldn't have young kids wearing beepers to school because it makes more sense to run drugs for someone than to take some of the jobs that are available. I don't know of any kid who is making money by running booze."

By undercutting the illegal drug trade, government could also drastically reduce the violence caused by drug sellers in bloody disputes over turf. Consequently, homicide rates would decline. Since drug users would no longer have to pay sky-high prices, they would resort less often to robbery and burglary to support their habits.

Advocates of legalization see additional advantages in following this policy. In each of the past few years, government expenditures on all aspects of drug enforcement — from drug eradication to imprisonment of dealers and users — totaled about $10 billion. Even the modest change of decriminalizing the possession of an ounce or less of marijuana results in substantial savings. In California, where such a policy has been in effect, state officials estimate that it has resulted in savings of close to $1 billion over the past decade. Because legalization means that fewer government enforcement efforts are necessary, it would result in substantial savings.

Moreover, if drugs were legalized, sales taxes on them would generate sufficient revenues to fund treatment and rehabilitation programs. If marijuana were taxed like cigarettes, it would generate an estimated $11 billion a year — ten times more than state and federal agencies currently spend each year on drug treatment.

Advocates of this choice conclude that devoting more resources to drug treatment would put the emphasis of America's anti-drug efforts in the right place. Rather than chasing drug users away by threatening to apply criminal sanctions, we should make every effort to identify them in order to provide treatment.

Like alcoholics, individuals who become dependent on drugs are sick people who deserve medical attention. It is both inhumane and irrational to punish them for behavior they cannot help. "We should constantly point out," says Arnold Trebach, "that drug users and abusers are members of our family, so to speak, and that we want to help, not punish them."

WHAT WORKS, WHAT'S RIGHT

In part, the argument for legalization is based upon certain convictions about what's right, about the ways in which laws that prohibit drug use infringe upon personal freedom.

In the words of policy analyst Ronald Hamowy, "This country was not founded on the principle that our governors are our parents, to whom we have entrusted the power to prevent us from harming ourselves. A truly liberal society cannot prevent some people from using drugs because a segment of the community condemns such pleasures any more than it can prohibit some of us from reading certain books because some portion of the population finds these works offensive. Defenders of criminalization cannot avoid the problem of how to reconcile these laws with a society based upon personal liberty and individual responsibility."

In another respect, the argument for legalization is based on certain assumptions about what is likely to work.

It reflects a pragmatic judgment about how to convince people to change bad habits.

Advocates of legalization conclude that a far more promising strategy than the current anti-drug policy is one that resembles the successful campaign against tobacco and alcohol — namely, a strategy that legalizes, controls, and discourages. Just as the repeal of Prohibition did not signal society's approval of alcohol, the legalization of drugs would not signal that anyone approves of drug use. All that the repeal of Prohibition signaled was our abandonment of a law enforcement strategy to contain and discourage the use of harmful substances.

In contrast to the position taken by advocates of "zero tolerance," proponents of legalization are persuaded that the goal of ridding society of drugs is an unattainable dream. Moreover, they are convinced that policymakers who try to achieve that goal will overlook measures that are more likely to help people kick the habit or keep people from using drugs in the first place.

"There is no final solution to the drug problem," writes attorney Kevin Zeese. "There will always be use and abuse of drugs, whatever the laws. If the laws are reformed, we will only be changing strategy, not surrendering. Ultimately, though, it will be easier to discourage drug abuse and treat drug users when we stop threatening to imprison them."

WHAT CRITICS SAY

Most politicians and policymakers regard legalization as a reckless and ill-conceived proposal. In the view of Senator Alfonse D'Amato, it would vastly increase the number of addicts and turn the United States into a "society of zombies."

To undercut the drug black market, government would have to substantially lower prices. Critics are convinced that if drugs were cheaper and more readily accessible, they would be more widely used. Currently, the cost of drugs, the difficulty of purchasing them, and the fear of legal sanctions deter many people from using them. If the legal stigma were removed, many law-abiding citizens would experiment with narcotics and a substantial number of them would get hooked.

After the repeal of Prohibition, there was a rapid increase in alcohol consumption and in the incidence of alcohol-related disease. The same thing might well happen if drugs were legalized, which would lead to a sharp increase in addiction and heightened demand for treatment and rehabilitation.

"If you want to get a flavor of what legalization would be like," said Representative Charles Rangel in his introduction to congressional hearings on this topic in 1988, "take this country's drug problem as it exists now and multiply it by two or three times. Addiction would rise dramatically. If we legalize drugs, we are asking for social chaos and disorder."

In particular, legalization might have a devastating effect on low-income, inner-city neighborhoods where drug use is especially prevalent. In the words of substance abuse specialists Karen Gorell and William Hendee, since minority communities and lower socioeconomic classes are particularly affected by the drug problem, "Legalization of drugs would be interpreted by these groups as a signal that their welfare is of little concern to the rest of society, so long as drug-related crime that extends into more affluent communities is reduced."

Critics point out that the effects of

THE CASE FOR LEGALIZING MARIJUANA

Some states have decriminalized marijuana. In New York, Ohio, California, Oregon, and seven other states, the possession of small amounts of marijuana is punishable by only a small fine. Elsewhere, it can result in prison sentences. Even where harsher laws remain on the books, however, enforcement officials generally put a low priority on making arrests for the possession of small amounts of marijuana and hashish.

Although customs officials might confiscate your car if you are caught bringing marijuana joints across the Mexican border, possession of small amounts of marijuana and hashish has, in effect, been decriminalized by local law enforcement officials in many parts of the country. The question is whether these substances should be declared legal and sold under the same kind of restrictions that apply to the sale of cigarettes and alcohol. Testifying before the House Select Committee on Narcotics in September 1988, Marvin D. Miller, attorney for the National Organization for the Reform of Marijuana Laws, made the case for legalizing marijuana. This passage is adapted from Miller's testimony.

Marijuana is the most widely used of all currently prohibited drugs. It is the one that has the least potential for abuse. Yet we expend the largest portion of our drug enforcement resources on the possession of marijuana, the most benign drug.

Lumping marijuana with crack/cocaine, heroin, and other more severe substances is as impractical as it is inaccurate. Marijuana is not addictive and does not exact the costs to our society as do other drugs such as alcohol and tobacco. A 1988 Surgeon General's report

IRA BLOCK/THE IMAGE BANK

listed tobacco as a more harmful drug than marijuana.

Marijuana is known as a drug which induces serenity rather than violence. Unlike PCP, it is not known to create violent behavior. It does not induce criminal activity, as do other drugs. Moreover, marijuana users do not commit other crimes to support their recreational use.

Americans who use marijuana are generally productive members of our society. Their only criminal association occurs because marijuana is a prohibited substance and its possession is a crime. Users are forced to have contact with and fuel the drug underground in order to obtain marijuana for their personal use.

They should not be cast out of society because they prefer marijuana to scotch, gin, or bourbon. Making millions of American citizens criminals does more harm than good.

When we tell young people about the harm of drugs, if we honestly admit that marijuana is not as harmful as other substances, something they already know, they will more likely listen to and believe us when we warn them about other drugs. To lump marijuana with hard drugs and treat all of them the same is not to tell the truth.

Everyone alters their consciousness. Some do it through alcohol, others through caffeine or nicotine, while some prefer fiction novels and fantasy movies. Others alter their consciousness through meditation or by the comfort of religion. People should be allowed to choose their own means of altering consciousness in the privacy of their own home.

Marijuana is a mild consciousness-altering substance that is nonaddictive and relatively nondeleterious compared to alcohol and tobacco. Its regulated availability ought to be allowed.

legalizing some drugs would be quite different from legalizing others. Legalizing cocaine, for example, would be more dangerous than legalizing marijuana. Heavy users of cocaine frequently exhibit violent behavior. Moreover, cocaine addicts tend to go on binges. Over time, users seek higher doses. Laboratory studies show that when animals are given unlimited amounts of cocaine, they use increasingly large doses and eventually die. Cheaper and more readily available cocaine is likely to lead to an increase in violent behavior as well as more frequent episodes of depression and paranoia.

Although some psychoactive drugs pose a greater danger than others, critics of legalization are convinced that all illicit drugs have deleterious effects — either physical or mental, or both. Though medical researchers differ about the damage caused by occasional use of marijuana, there is some agreement about the dangers associated with prolonged, regular use, particularly to the lungs and to short-term memory. Like alcohol, marijuana use impairs perception, coordination, and memory. THC, the active ingredient, lowers the concentration of reproductive hormones in the bloodstream.

Each of these health effects is especially serious for young people, which critics of this proposal regard as an additional reason for concern about legalizing drugs. Experience with alcohol and tobacco suggests that even if the sale of drugs is strictly regulated and sales to minors are prohibited, legal access for adults would permit minors to get drugs too.

Because drugs are harmful not only to individual users but also to the community, those who oppose legalization conclude that society *must* control them and make every effort to

RICHARD SMART, AUTHOR

I WENT FROM HOT-SHOT LAWYER TO COCAINE ADDICT.

And I didn't just ruin myself, I spread disaster among my family, friends and business associates. And for years I denied the addiction—until the money was gone—and my jet set life totally blown away. Not a dime left—not an ounce of self-respect. Anybody tells you cocaine isn't addictive is a liar.

COCAINE. THE BIG LIE. 1-800-662-HELP.

THE ADVERTISING COUNCIL, INC.

prohibit their use. This is not an area in which it is appropriate for individuals to decide for themselves.

Furthermore, opponents doubt that legalization would wipe out drug-related crime. Unless government permitted the purchase of unlimited quantities of narcotics anonymously — a procedure that few people are willing to accept — a drug black market would continue to operate.

If drugs were legalized, users would still need money to support their habits. If the number of addicts increased, drug-related violence would increase too. "Does anyone really think," asks Representative Benjamin

Gilman, "that under legalization the crack addict is going to go into a drug supermarket, pick up a legal dosage of crack and then stay out of trouble? I don't think so."

THE WRONG MESSAGE

Critics of legalization are also concerned that lowering the legal barrier sends the wrong message about society's attitude toward drugs. Opponents of legalization are concerned that no matter how often public figures explained that they do not condone drug use, legalization of illicit substances would be interpreted as a green light on drugs, and that message would overwhelm educational efforts to underscore the dangers of drug use.

Legalization, says psychiatrist Robert Coles, "would amount to moral surrender." Coles fears that legalization would be widely interpreted as permission to ignore the consequences of one's behavior. "I'm not prepared as a parent, as a citizen, or as a doctor to say that," he says.

Even proponents of legalization admit that no one knows to what extent legalization would reduce crime or increase addiction. For that reason, critics conclude that legalization is a very risky experiment. "What if there were a fifty-fold increase in the number of those dependent on cocaine?" asks John Kaplan. "We simply cannot guarantee that such a situation would not come to pass. Since we cannot do so, it is the height of irresponsibility to advocate risking the future of the nation."

The question is whether, in Representative Rangel's words, legalization amounts to nothing more than "idle chitchat," a proposal that would have devastating results if put into effect. Or does it offer a promising alternative, a radically different way to come to grips with an apparently intractable problem?■

FIGHTING DRUGS: STRATEGIES AND SOLUTIONS

"While a consensus has developed about the importance of expanded anti-drug efforts, there is no agreement about what should be done."

In the United States, where 23 million people regularly use illicit substances, the drug problem is very much on people's minds. Early in 1989, New York Governor Mario Cuomo called drug abuse "the single most ominous phenomenon of our times" and promised that it would be at the top of the state's agenda. A *New York Times* poll taken on the eve of the Bush administration showed that the public agrees that drugs are the nation's number one problem.

"There is a sense developing," says David Musto, an authority on drug abuse, "that we cannot go on like this. What you are seeing is a sign that a consensus has developed in America that the drug problem is intolerable."

No President spoke out against drugs more often than Ronald Reagan. No administration spent more to stem the flow of drugs into the country. Still, as the Reagan administration ended, most law enforcement officials acknowledged that they were fighting a losing battle.

Polls show that the American public is not optimistic that the new administration will do any better. Despite President Bush's insistence in his Inaugural Address that "this scourge will stop," a *New York Times* poll showed that just 35 percent of a nationwide sample believed that the new administration would be able to significantly reduce the drug problem.

Although the drug situation is very serious, it isn't entirely bleak. The good news is that demand for drugs — at least among young middle-class Americans — seems to be declining. A 1987 survey of high school students, for example, shows a drop in the number of students who said they had used illicit drugs — down to 50 percent from almost 60 percent in 1984.

The bad news is that the problem gets worse as you move down the social scale. Among young people in poor neighborhoods, the use of crack seems to be on the rise. Since drug use takes an especially high toll in the inner cities, whatever anti-drug strategy we choose had better be responsive to the needs of Americans who live in poor urban communities.

COMMITMENTS AND CONSTRAINTS

What is at issue in the drug debate? In one respect, the question is how to devote sufficient resources to anti-drug efforts. While elected officials at the state and federal level reaffirm their commitment to combat drugs, budgetary constraints keep officials from responding adequately to the demand for law enforcement and drug treatment facilities.

In New York State, for example, although the governor's proposed budget would provide treatment facilities for an additional 5,500 cocaine and heroin addicts, the plan falls far short of providing treatment to "every individual who needs and wants it," as the governor urged.

Similarly, although New York State is devoting increasing amounts to law enforcement efforts to stem the drug problem, the problem is growing faster than the criminal justice system is expanding. Statewide, felony drug arrests have risen by more than 110 percent over the past four years, indictments have tripled, and convictions have doubled.

One reason choices have to be made among anti-drug strategies is that each of these strategies, if pursued seriously, requires a substantial commitment of public funds. A plan to step up international efforts to stop the production of drugs, for example, would

DAN WASSERMAN, THE LOS ANGELES TIMES SYNDICATE

require a massive foreign aid effort to encourage the cultivation of other marketable crops and to promote economic development in drug-producing nations. A serious interdiction effort would require posting thousands of additional personnel along the borders, as well as hiring thousands of additional Customs officials. Similarly, a domestic enforcement strategy would require a massive infusion of resources into the criminal justice system. Since drug treatment — which is favored by advocates of the third and fourth approaches — costs a minimum of several thousand dollars per person each year, providing such treatment for every individual who wants and needs it would require far more public resources than are currently spent for this purpose. To pursue several strategies simultaneously would require more resources than elected officials are able to commit for anti-drug efforts.

CHOOSING A STRATEGY

In a deeper sense, the problem is deciding what should be done to fight drugs. If a public consensus has developed about the importance of expanded anti-drug efforts, there is as yet no consensus about which of several strategies is most likely to be effective.

When polls ask what measures are likely to reduce drug use a great deal — such as stiffer penalties for users, military raids on drug producers abroad, or providing additional drug treatment programs — no measure receives majority support. Although drug testing in the workplace is regarded as one of the most promising proposals, there is widespread concern about the invasion of privacy that testing entails.

We could, of course, get tougher on drug traffickers, sellers, and users. In Malaysia, drug trafficking is punished by hanging. In Iran, harsh new laws require the death sentence for anyone

caught carrying more than an ounce of most drugs. Individuals who are responsible for addicting others face a minimum prison sentence of 20 years. The question is how far most Americans are willing to go with drug law enforcement. The task is to develop a policy that is consistent with American concepts of civil liberties and just punishment.

CHOICES AND CONSEQUENCES

As a nation, we face clear choices about drug policy. As in other areas, the choices that are most popular are not necessarily the most effective. Take drug education, for example. "If demand is the problem," writes drug policy expert, Mark Kleiman, "then education must be the solution, right? Yes, but that doesn't mean we know how to do it. Random anti-drug messages do more harm than good. So if somebody offers you a cute advertising program without clear evidence of its effectiveness, just say no."

Each of the alternatives imposes substantial costs. We might conclude, as President Reagan did in 1981, that it is "virtually impossible" to halt drugs at the border because "it's like carrying water in a sieve." That leads some people to the conclusion that the nation should concentrate enforcement on domestic drug markets.

If that is the main direction for anti-drug efforts, we have a choice. Should law enforcement officials concentrate on the illegal drugs that cause the most harm to users and cause the most crime? If so, it would mean abandoning efforts to deter marijuana use. If not, it would require a vast expansion of existing law enforcement efforts and the apprehension of millions of people who use marijuana, but not other drugs.

Knowing that what drug dealers really fear is being jailed, we could concentrate on putting dealers behind bars. But if we want to use a domestic enforcement strategy to control the drug problem, we should be prepared, according to the best estimates, to double the size of the federal prison system and build 50,000 additional federal prison cells.

We could substantially expand random testing to deter use and send the signal that drug use will not be tolerated. But that means turning schools and employers into enforcement agencies and permitting a procedure that amounts to a blatant invasion of privacy. Moreover, it poses a question: Does it make sense to conduct random searches in order to identify (and punish) individuals whose drug use does not affect their performance on the job or at school?

To cut down on drug-related crime, we could legalize certain drugs. But are we willing to risk the possibility of significantly increased drug use, and a significant rise in addiction?

One of the goals of public debate about drugs should be to reach a consensus about which measures are most likely to reduce drug use, and which are consistent with the other things we value. Not incidentally, we need to consider whether we're prepared to live with the consequences of those choices.

HABITS OF SPEECH

What people decide to do about anti-drug efforts depends in large part on how they think and talk about them. If this is *war*, it may make sense to escalate the effort until the enemy is subdued. It may be, as Representative Charles Rangel said, that the reason why America's anti-drug efforts have not been notably successful is that elected officials have "refused to provide the money and leadership to fight a real war on drugs."

TEENAGE DRUG ABUSE: HOW ONE COMMUNITY RESPONDED

When Kent, a high school junior in a Cleveland suburb, admitted that he used drugs and alcohol, his parents responded angrily. Kent's father, who knew very little about addiction, responded to his son's drug use not as a medical problem but as a behavior problem. His first reaction was to impose stricter rules and tighter curfews.

Kent regarded his father's response as a form of punishment for admitting that he used drugs. As Kent's self-esteem deteriorated, so did communication with his parents. It wasn't until Kent was rushed to the hospital after overdosing on drugs that his parents reexamined their views about addiction.

Soon after, Kent was admitted to a nearby hospital-based drug treatment program. His parents started attending parenting groups and enrolled in a family counseling program. With the help of his parents, as well as doctors and counselors, Kent overcame his drug problem. His parents credit the community's drug-abuse support system for helping them deal with Kent's addiction and cope successfully with the family problems it created.

In several respects, Cleveland's community-based response to teenage drug abuse is a model of what can be done when parents, schools, community leaders, and religious organizations team up with professional drug counselors and treatment facilities. Responding to the local drug crisis, this network of individuals and organizations has mounted a multifaceted effort:

- Many Cleveland-area schools now offer drug counseling as well as referral programs that encourage family involvement.
- Church, school, and parent groups organized programs to discourage drug use.
- Citizens solicited the assistance of businesses and public agencies in establishing drug treatment facilities and halfway houses for recovering teenage drug abusers.
- Juvenile courts worked with parents and counselors to establish new rehabilitation alternatives for drug-related offenses.
- The media encouraged the entire effort by publicizing anti-drug organizations and activities.

Although Cleveland's response to the problem of teenage drug abuse is unusually comprehensive, many communities are mounting anti-drug abuse efforts:

- In several New York City suburbs, law enforcement officers train citizens in Neighborhood Watch groups to watch for and report drug dealing.
- In Los Angeles, businessmen deliberately hire gang members to steer them away from drug dealing and drug use.
- In Atlanta, an organization known as 100 Black Men adopted an eighth grade class in an inner-city school. Each member of the organization serves as mentor to a particular student and promises to send that student to college if he or she graduates from high school and stays away from drugs.

THE DRUG PROBLEM?... THAT'S EASY. JUST SAY...

YES!

POLITICIANS

ANTI-DRUG BANDWAGON

DANA SUMMERS, *THE ORLANDO SENTINEL*

Faced with a clear public menace, it may be appropriate — as in wartime — to suspend or curtail certain civil liberties, or to modify normal procedural rules for law enforcement officials in order to wage war effectively. Perhaps, as New York's Mayor Koch suggests, we should strip search every person who enters the United States from Mexico or Southeast Asia. Perhaps the Customs Service should have the authority it requested to "use appropriate force" to compel planes suspected of carrying drugs to land, including the authority to shoot them down. Perhaps it is appropriate to comply with the request of the Council of D.C. for National Guard troops to occupy certain neighborhoods where the drug trade has overwhelmed local enforcement officials. If we are to wage an effective war on drugs, such measures — as unappealing as they sound — may be necessary.

Others who regard the drug issue as a *moral* matter conclude that "zero tolerance" is the only defensible approach. From this perspective, it is morally offensive to permit a policy of compromise such as the Dutch solution, which offers an outlet to people who wish to experiment with soft drugs while outlawing more addictive substances. As we have seen, some people regard that approach as a pragmatic and promising way to break the spiral of addiction. To those who regard the anti-drug effort as a moral matter, however, a compromise of this sort amounts to capitulation.

Still others who think about drug use primarily as a *medical* problem choose a different course of action. From their perspective, the Surgeon General, rather than the Attorney General, should lead federal anti-drug efforts. Rather than devoting additional public resources to identifying and punishing drug users, our chief concern should be to provide treatment to help users overcome their dependency.

In the words of Karst Besteman, executive director of the Alcohol and Drug Problems Association, talking about a "war on drugs" leads to confused thinking and inappropriate responses. "You don't fight a war with treatment," he says. "Talking about war and toughness is just not compatible with a discussion of human needs. We won't really solve the drug problem and support worthwhile programs unless we drop this silliness."

In this sense, the first question in the drug debate is how we choose to talk about it. For all the talk about "waging a war on drugs" and trying to achieve a "drug-free America," the most sensible and effective policy may have the more modest goal of reducing the damage drug users do to themselves and to other people.

The drug debate is about pushers and drug trafficking, users and abuse, prevention and enforcement. It is about public policies — including drug education, testing, and applying the death penalty for drug pushers. In a deeper sense, it is about law and order, about what government should be permitted to do to stop individuals from practicing a pernicious habit.

During the course of congressional deliberations about the 1988 Anti-Drug Abuse Act, several observers noted that for all the concern about drugs and posturing about the need for a "tough" drug policy, there was little debate about which anti-drug strategy makes the most sense. In the words of drug expert Peter Reuter, "There is no debate taking place in Congress about the fundamental issues. At best, we're just beginning to have a debate about having a debate." The goal of these Forums is to invite debate about how to deal with one of the nation's most pressing problems. ■

For Further Reading

A useful overview of federal drug policies can be found in a report entitled *1984 National Strategy for Prevention of Drug Abuse and Drug Trafficking* (Washington, DC: Drug Abuse Policy Office, The White House, 1984). For a brief summary of the debate surrounding these policies, see "Drug Control," a Congressional Research Service issue brief by Harry Hogan (Washington, DC: C.R.S., 1988). The National Institute on Drug Abuse compiles statistical profiles on drug use: "The National Household Survey on Drug Abuse: Main Findings, 1985" and "The National High School Senior Survey on Drug Abuse: 1987" (Rockville, MD: NIDA, 1987).

"Drug Control: International Policy and Options," another recent Congressional Research Service publication, written by Raphael F. Perl and Roy Surrett (Washington, DC: C.R.S., 1988), provides a summary of efforts to control the drug problem at the source. Edward I. Koch makes the argument for increasing international efforts to fight the drug problem in an article entitled "Declaring War on Drugs," *Conservative Digest* (August 1985).

For the argument against an international war on drugs, see Peter Reuter, "Can the Borders Be Sealed?" *The Public Interest* (Summer 1988). Elaine Shannon's account of the 1985 murder of a DEA agent in Mexico, entitled *Desperados: Latin Drug Lords, U.S. Lawmen and the War America Can't Win* (New York: Viking Press, 1988), provides a vivid description of efforts to stem international drug production.

The U.S. National Drug Enforcement Policy Board publishes an annual *Federal Drug Enforcement Progress*

ROB SAUNDERS

Report (Washington, DC: Government Printing Office, 1986), which details how increased enforcement efforts help curb drug dealing in the United States. For an analysis of the issues surrounding crackdowns on local drug dealers, see *Street-Level Drug Enforcement: Examining the Issues*, edited by Marcia R. Chaiken (Washington, DC: National Institute of Justice, U.S. Department of Justice, 1988).

The controversy surrounding employee drug testing is summarized in a Congressional Research Service publication, "Drug Testing in the Workplace: An Overview of Employee and Employer Interests," by Gail McCallion (Washington, DC: C.R.S., 1988). The American Civil Liberties Union publishes several pamphlets that explain the argument against random drug testing from a civil libertarian perspective. See, for example, the A.C.L.U.'s briefing paper, "Drug Testing in the Workplace."

For a critical view of current drug policies, see Ronald Hamowy, ed., *Dealing with Drugs: Consequences of Government Control* (Lexington, MA: Lexington Books, 1987). In *Drug Control in a Free Society* (New York: Cambridge University Press, 1985), James B. Bakalar and Lester Grinspoon argue that America's drug laws are incompatible with our emphasis on individual freedom.

Ethan A. Nadelmann makes the argument for legalizing drugs in "The Case for Legalization," *The Public*

Interest (Summer 1988). John Kaplan's *Marijuana, the New Prohibition* (New York: Crowell, 1975) presents the case for legalizing marijuana.

For community and school-based approaches to the drug problem, see *What Works: Schools Without Drugs* (Washington, DC: U.S. Department of Education, 1987) and *Epidemic in Retreat: A Community Response to Teenage Drug Abuse* by Jean M. Buchannan (Glenbeigh Institute, 1984).

Acknowledgments

Many people participated in the process of deciding upon this year's topics, discussing how they should be approached, and preparing the materials. Once again this year, David Mathews and Daniel Yankelovich provided both guidance and support. Jon Rye Kinghorn played a vital role in providing assistance to the convening institutions and Forum leaders.

For their advice and assistance in sharpening the arguments contained in this booklet, we are grateful to our consultants: Robert DuPont, psychiatrist and former director of the National Institute on Drug Abuse; Mark Kleiman, lecturer on criminal justice at the John F. Kennedy School at Harvard University; Ethan Nadelmann, assistant professor at the Woodrow Wilson School at Princeton University; and Peter Reuter, senior economist at the Rand Corporation. In addition, our colleagues John Doble, Jean Johnson, Jon Rye Kinghorn, Robert Kingston, Suzanne Morse, Pat Scully, Jeffrey Tuchman, and Deborah Wadsworth helped to refine the framework and to clarify the argument.

NATIONAL ISSUES FORUMS

The National Issues Forums (NIF) program consists of locally initiated Forums and study circles which bring citizens together in communities throughout the nation for nonpartisan discussions about public issues. In these Forums, the traditional town meeting concept is re-created. Each fall and winter, three issues of particular concern are addressed in these groups. The results are then shared with policymakers.

More than a thousand civic and education organizations — high schools and colleges, libraries, service organizations, religious groups, and other types of groups — convene Forums and study circles in their communities as part of the National Issues Forums. Each participating organization assumes ownership of the program, adapting the NIF approach and materials to its own mission and to the needs of the local community. In this sense, there is no one type of NIF program. There are many varieties, all locally directed and financed.

Here are answers to some of the most frequently asked questions about the National Issues Forums:

"WHAT HAPPENS IN FORUMS?"

The goal of Forums and study circles is to stimulate and sustain a certain kind of conversation — a genuinely useful conversation that moves beyond the bounds of partisan politics and the airing of grievances to mutually acceptable responses to common problems. Distinctively, Forums invite discussion about each of several choices, along with their cost and the main arguments for and against them. Forum moderators encourage participants to examine their values and preferences — as individuals and as community members — and apply them to specific issues.

"CAN I PARTICIPATE IF I'M NOT WELL INFORMED ABOUT THE ISSUE?"

To discuss public issues, citizens need to grasp the underlying problem or dilemma, and they should understand certain basic facts and trends. But it isn't necessary to know a great deal about an issue. NIF discussions focus on what public actions should be taken. That's a matter of judgment that requires collective deliberation. The most important thing to ponder and discuss is the kernel of convictions on which each alternative is based. The task of the National Issues Forums is not to help participants acquire a detailed knowledge of the issue but to help people sort out conflicting principles and preferences, to find out where they agree and disagree and work toward common understandings.

"ISN'T ONE PERSON'S OPINION AS GOOD AS ANOTHER'S?"

Public judgment differs from personal opinion. It arises when people sort out their values and work through hard choices. Public judgment reflects people's views once they have an opportunity to confront an issue seriously, consider the arguments for and against various positions, and come to terms with the consequences of their beliefs.

"ARE FORUM PARTICIPANTS EXPECTED TO AGREE UPON A COURSE OF ACTION?"

A fundamental challenge in a democratic nation is sustaining a consensus about a broad direction of public action without ignoring or denying the diversity of individual preferences. Forums do not attempt to achieve complete agreement. Rather, their goal is to help people see which interests are shareable and which are not. A Forum moderator once described the common ground in these words: "Here are five statements that were made in our community Forum. Not everyone agreed with all of them. But there is nothing in them that we couldn't agree with."

"WHAT'S THE POINT OF ONE MORE BULL SESSION?"

Making choices is hard work. It requires something more than talking about public issues. "Talking about" is what we do every day. We talk about the weather, or our friends, or the government. But the "choice work" that takes place in Forum discussions involves weighing alternatives and considering the consequences of various courses of action. It means accepting certain choices even if they aren't entirely consistent with what we want, and even if the cost is higher than we imagined. Forum participants learn how to work through issues together. That means using talk to discover, not just to persuade or advocate.

"DO THE FORUMS LEAD TO POLITICAL ACTION?"

Neither local convenors nor the National Issues Forums as a whole advocate partisan positions or specific solutions. The Forums' purpose is to influence the political process in a more fundamental way. Before elected officials decide upon specific proposals, they need to know what kinds of initiatives the public favors. As President Carter once said, "Government cannot set our goals and it cannot define our vision." The purpose of the Forums is to provide an occasion for people to decide what broad direction public action should take.

THE DRUG CRISIS: PUBLIC STRATEGIES FOR BREAKING THE HABIT

One of the reasons people participate in the National Issues Forums is that they want leaders to know how they feel about the issues. So that we can present your thoughts and feelings about this issue, we'd like you to fill out this ballot before you attend Forum meetings (or before you read this book, if you buy it elsewhere), and a second ballot after the Forum (or after you've read the material).

The moderator of your local Forum will ask you to hand in this ballot at the end of the session. If you cannot attend the meeting, send the completed ballot to National Issues Forums, 100 Commons Road, Dayton, Ohio 45459-2777.

		Worse	About the Same	Better	Not Sure
1.	Compared to five years ago, do you feel the *nation's* illegal drug problem is getting worse, staying about the same, or getting better?	☐	☐	☐	☐
2.	Compared to five years ago, do you think the drug problem in *your community* is getting worse, staying about the same, or getting better?	☐	☐	☐	☐

3. Here are some proposals to combat the drug problem. Indicate which of the following, if any, you support.

		Favor	Oppose	Not Sure
a.	Give aid to South American and Asian farmers as an incentive to stop growing drug crops, even if this proves to be very costly to U.S. taxpayers	☐	☐	☐
b.	Impose sanctions on South American and Asian countries that tolerate the drug industry, even if it angers friendly countries, pushing them toward communism	☐	☐	☐
c.	Greatly step up border patrols to stop the flow of drugs, even if this is expensive and intercepts only a small fraction of the supply	☐	☐	☐
d.	Use the U.S. military to patrol our borders and enforce drug laws, even if this requires new equipment and diverts the military from its main role	☐	☐	☐
e.	Expand police forces in order to arrest more drug dealers, even if other dealers quickly fill the places of those arrested	☐	☐	☐
f.	Let the police search the homes of suspected drug dealers without a warrant, even if the homes of innocent people are sometimes searched by mistake	☐	☐	☐
g.	Arrest and prosecute small-time drug dealers, even if this clogs the courts, delays trials for cases involving violent crimes, and requires building more prisons	☐	☐	☐
h.	Impose the death penalty on drug dealers who are responsible for drug-related murders, even if many people are morally opposed to capital punishment	☐	☐	☐

		Favor	Oppose	Not Sure
i.	Encourage private companies to conduct random drug tests on their employees, even if many people feel that drug testing is an invasion of privacy	☐	☐	☐
j.	Impose harsher penalties on *all* identified drug users, even if that means prison sentences and heavy fines for occasional marijuana users	☐	☐	☐
k.	Provide immediate drug treatment for anyone who needs it, even if this is very costly	☐	☐	☐
l.	Legalize marijuana, even if changing the law appears to condone the use of a harmful drug	☐	☐	☐
m.	Legalize cocaine and heroin and regulate their use, even if this increases the availability of these drugs and leads to more addiction, especially in inner-city areas	☐	☐	☐

4. Several different ways to fight illegal drugs have been proposed. Rate how effective each would be on a scale of 1 to 7, where "1" means it would be ineffective in reducing illegal drug use and "7" means it would be very effective in reducing illegal drug use.

1 to 7

a. Attack drugs at their source through crop eradication, sanctions against countries that tolerate drug trafficking, and aid to South American and Asian farmers who stop producing drugs _____

b. Crack down on domestic dealers through increased police patrols and searches of homes and harsher penalties for drug sellers _____

c. Crack down on drug users through harsher penalties and widespread mandatory testing _____

d. Reduce the demand for drugs by expanding drug treatment facilities and anti-drug educational campaigns _____

e. Legalize drugs and regulate their sale to adults _____

5. Which of these age groups are you in?
☐ Under 18   ☐ 18-29   ☐ 30-44   ☐ 45-64   ☐ Over 65

6. Are you a   ☐ Man   ☐ Woman

7. What is your ZIP code? _____

POST-FORUM BALLOT

THE DRUG CRISIS: PUBLIC STRATEGIES FOR BREAKING THE HABIT

Now that you've had a chance to read the book or attend a Forum discussion we'd like to know what you think about this issue. Your opinions, along with those of thousands of others who participated in this year's Forums, will be reflected in a summary report prepared for participants as well as elected officials and policymakers working on this problem. Since we're interested in whether you have changed your mind about certain aspects of this issue, the questions are the same as those you answered earlier.

Please hand this ballot to the Forum leader at the end of the session, or mail it to National Issues Forums, 100 Commons Road, Dayton, Ohio 45459-2777.

1. Compared to five years ago, do you feel the *nation's* illegal drug problem is getting worse, staying about the same, or getting better?

Worse	About the Same	Better	Not Sure
☐	☐	☐	☐

2. Compared to five years ago, do you think the drug problem in *your community* is getting worse, staying about the same, or getting better?

Worse	About the Same	Better	Not Sure
☐	☐	☐	☐

3. Here are some proposals to combat the drug problem. Indicate which of the following, if any, you support.

	Favor	Oppose	Not Sure
a. Give aid to South American and Asian farmers as an incentive to stop growing drug crops, even if this proves to be very costly to U.S. taxpayers	☐	☐	☐
b. Impose sanctions on South American and Asian countries that tolerate the drug industry, even if it angers friendly countries, pushing them toward communism	☐	☐	☐
c. Greatly step up border patrols to stop the flow of drugs, even if this is expensive and intercepts only a small fraction of the supply	☐	☐	☐
d. Use the U.S. military to patrol our borders and enforce drug laws, even if this requires new equipment and diverts the military from its main role	☐	☐	☐
e. Expand police forces in order to arrest more drug dealers, even if other dealers quickly fill the places of those arrested	☐	☐	☐
f. Let the police search the homes of suspected drug dealers without a warrant, even if the homes of innocent people are sometimes searched by mistake	☐	☐	☐
g. Arrest and prosecute small-time drug dealers, even if this clogs the courts, delays trials for cases involving violent crimes, and requires building more prisons	☐	☐	☐
h. Impose the death penalty on drug dealers who are responsible for drug-related murders, even if many people are morally opposed to capital punishment	☐	☐	☐

NATIONAL ISSUES FORUMS

(over)

		Favor	Oppose	Not Sure
i.	Encourage private companies to conduct random drug tests on their employees, even if many people feel that drug testing is an invasion of privacy	☐	☐	☐
j.	Impose harsher penalties on *all* identified drug users, even if that means prison sentences and heavy fines for occasional marijuana users	☐	☐	☐
k.	Provide immediate drug treatment for anyone who needs it, even if this is very costly	☐	☐	☐
l.	Legalize marijuana, even if changing the law appears to condone the use of a harmful drug	☐	☐	☐
m.	Legalize cocaine and heroin and regulate their use, even if this increases the availability of these drugs and leads to more addiction, especially in inner-city areas	☐	☐	☐

4. Several different ways to fight illegal drugs have been proposed. Rate how effective each would be on a scale of 1 to 7, where "1" means it would be ineffective in reducing illegal drug use and "7" means it would be very effective in reducing illegal drug use.

1 to 7

a. Attack drugs at their source through crop eradication, sanctions against countries that tolerate drug trafficking, and aid to South American and Asian farmers who stop producing drugs _____

b. Crack down on domestic dealers through increased police patrols and searches of homes and harsher penalties for drug sellers _____

c. Crack down on drug users through harsher penalties and widespread mandatory testing _____

d. Reduce the demand for drugs by expanding drug treatment facilities and anti-drug educational campaigns _____

e. Legalize drugs and regulate their sale to adults _____

5. Which of these age groups are you in?
☐ Under 18   ☐ 18-29   ☐ 30-44   ☐ 45-64   ☐ Over 65

6. Are you a   ☐ Man   ☐ Woman

7. What is your ZIP code? _____

8. We'd like to know whether, as you read this book and attended the Forums, you changed your mind about the drug crisis and how to break the nation's drug habit. How, if at all, did you change your mind?

9. If there were just one message you could send to elected leaders on the topic of the drug crisis, what would it be?